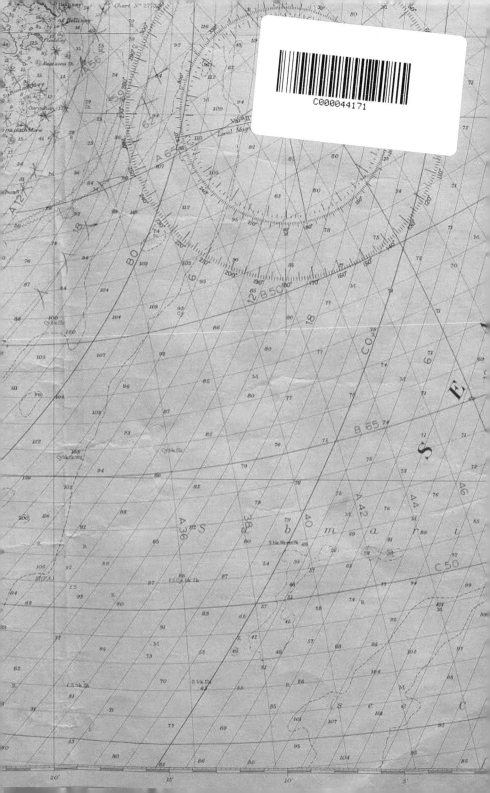

Shemaron:
A Beautiful Endeavour

Mascot Books

560 Herndon Parkway #120

Herndon, VA 20170

info@mascotbooks.com

PRTWP1015A

Library of Congress Control Number: 2015910015

ISBN-13: 9781631771507

www.mascotbooks.com

I have tried to recreate events, locales and conversations from my memories of them. I may have changed some identifying characteristics and details such as physical properties, occupations and places of residence.

Printed in Malaysia

SHEMARON

A Beautiful Endeavour

FIONA MALKIN

Acknowledgements

To my husband Christopher Malkin who I wish to commend for his effort in raising awareness of the ring net era and for his constant drive in preserving the ring net boat Shemaron CN244 formerly Wistaria BA64; also for access to the voice recordings he made and other conversations with ring net fishermen we have enjoyed together.

I have spent many hours trying to appropriately credit the carefully chosen photographs reproduced in this book, sadly I have not been able to in every case as many of them were taken over 50 years ago. I would ask for the reader's indulgence on this matter.

Bringing the information together for this book has involved many conversations, sometimes over the telephone and sometimes in person. The quest for knowledge was met with good humor, encouragement and a happy willingness to talk whatever the time of day. The practical advice and guidance received towards handling and renovating Shemaron has been greatly appreciated. My thanks

extend to people from the island of Gigha, to the towns
and villages of Campbeltown, Carradale and Tarbert, across the
Clyde to Ayr, Troon and Dunure and over to the North East coast to
people from Lundin Links on the Firth of Forth, St. Abbs, Eyemouth,
Seahouses and Sunderland.

Introduction

I have always enjoyed listening to stories; I like the way words flow together and conjure images. I have used them and written them until this point on a casual basis, trying to capture moods and memories for my own satisfaction. However, I found the experience of spending time onboard an old fishing boat fascinating, and it provided me with a subject so amazing that I could not have done it justice within my usual writing scope. To set it down on paper has been a most enjoyable challenge. I allowed myself the luxury of writing by instinct; I felt encouraged by the freedom this approach allowed. This meant that I had to keep re-adjusting the text whenever I came upon an interesting fact, or recognised a new facet to the ring net story; I was like a sculptor, or artist capturing a changing expression.

The ring net stories that came to me in such an enjoyable manner during conversations with ex-ring net men caught my imagination. They were relayed with enthusiasm and were responsible for adding so much colour and texture to my view of Shemaron. I have included them here in the free spirit in which they were given. Some of the stories may have been recorded before, as there have been some excellent books written about the ring net era.

The early ring net boats were built for a world I had yet to come to. I have somehow found myself at the wrong end of the ring net story, standing quite literally, under its bows; trying to catch the frayed threads of it before it unravels too far for me to draw them together again. So many boats have been decommissioned, literally broken up; others have come to other sad ends. However, it is because of this regrettable situation that the few remaining boats have become so important to our heritage.

This book is not intended to be a history of the ring net, although history inevitably features to a large extent. Becoming involved with our ring net boat drew me into her story on a personal level; the accounts I heard brought her past to life. Her history eventually became an inseparable part of the whole experience. Excursions round Kintyre and the west coast of Scotland enabled me to add my own sense of place to the stories I had heard; combined with my own fresh adventure on the ocean, a potent mix began to brew. It eventually became clear to me that history, romance, poetry, and risk blended to form a heightened experience.

Shemaron: A Beautiful Endeavour is the story of the old ring net fishing boat formerly known as Wistaria BA64. The impact she had on my comfortable urban lifestyle was totally unexpected. I sailed away with her, and by the time I returned, we had bonded on an intimate level. I had learned much about her life and the industry for which she was built, the pursuit of herring with the ring net. My experience with Shemaron opened a portal through which I could step back in time and allow the past to mix with the present as I tried to understand what it was like to be a ring net fisherman. It is a story based around the western Scottish coast where the ring net first emerged as a method of catching herring. It blends together the beauty of the western seas and the historical record of a well-known Scottish ring net boat.

Chapter 1
The Sea

The Scottish seas have given rise to many highlights in my life. The sea has given me experiences through which I have pushed the boundaries of my horizons; the ends of days when I have rolled exhausted into my bunk, held safe in oak and rocked to sleep on the tilt of the tide; the early mornings when I have risen to a fresh, lonely world, then steamed through the pre-dawn dusk as colour gradually defined the coast. It is the ability to be part of the balance, bearing witness to nature in such a timeless manner, that elates me. Through that ability I can engage in those long, peaceful, perfect moments held in sighs and locked in memories.

Of all the things I could choose to do, one thing that absolutely never entered my head was that I would one day have anything to do with an old fishing trawler. This came about because my husband had a dream and his drive and enthusiasm in pursuit of this dream has seen us to the point of actually owning an old boat. Even though I could accept that this might happen for him, the idea that I would be involved in the experience at all, let alone enjoy it, was far from any future I had imagined. The acceptance that this was going to happen for him was very neatly compartmented in my head, inside a box with a closed lid, labelled "Chris' life".

I was never a person who knew where she wanted to be; rather, I took all that life threw at me and tried to make the best of every situation. I suppose if I saw anything in the future at all, it was probably running our business for as long as possible, hopefully followed in later years by a fewer number of commitments mingled with tea and scones, lunch with the girls, shopping trips, and a couple of slightly exotic and unusual holidays every now and again. It failed totally to connect with anything to do with a fishing trawler built in 1949. In retrospect, this vision of my future seemed more than a little mundane.

My teas, scones, and lunches with the girls have been replaced by invitations to refreshments around the hearths of ex-skippers, crew, and any person wishing to reminisce about the old days of the herring fishery. Although not much of a talker, I am fascinated with the banter and stories, which have opened up a whole new, previously unacknowledged interest. The beauty of it all is that it just keeps growing. Our boat, Shemaron, has an intriguing social history, and through the research of her past lives, I have grown to know her extremely well. The name Shemaron replaced her original name of Wistaria and is a joining of the names Sheila and Marion, mother and sister of Sandy Galbraith who was the last person to fish with her. The road to all things Shemaron has been so well camouflaged that I never quite realised I was travelling upon it; I was unwittingly becoming enmeshed in the world of our beautiful old boat.

One of the things I find so striking about fishermen is the love and passion they display towards the boats they worked on. They recall with ease the names and circumstance of various boats, like they are members of an extended family. Looking back sixty-odd years and remembering a first car just isn't the same; nostalgia is there to a degree with a car, but I think something runs much deeper with these men and I wonder what it was really like to be fishing for herring, or "at the herring".

The names of these beautiful old boats reflect a romance that is ever present on the lonely Scottish seas. The New Dawn, Rolling Wave, and Fair Morn could almost tell a story in their own right. As could the Storm Drift, Brighter Hope, Maid of the Mist, and Golden West. The beautifully sensuous names of these boats, their partnership with the sea, and the poetry they inspire, must be a reflection of many beautiful moments captured from their decks.

Shemaron sleeps seven, which meant up to seven crew members at a time were away, sometimes for many weeks, sharing a confined working and living space. These men must have respected each other, and would have trusted one another readily; they would have had to, given the dangerous conditions they worked in. Ring net boats worked in pairs, coming together after shooting their nets to haul in their catch, a partnership at sea that required strong bonds. I wondered also about the boats themselves. There is something very comforting about wood, being surrounded by it and cocooned within it. Sleeping on Shemaron is an unparalleled experience: in the soft light with the paraffin lamps swaying, the wooden interior warms and glows and the brass handrail flickers with shadows from the stove. The fo'c'sle is very comfortable. There was obviously a lot of pride and care taken in the upkeep of one's boat. Fo'c'sle is an abbreviated form of the original word forecastle which referred to the castle like structure at the front of old sailing ships. These days it generally refers to the forward living accommodation on boats; on Shemaron the fo'c'sle is the forward third of the boat.

I imagine Shemaron and similar boats on big seas. These must have been humbling experiences for skipper and crew. The vastness of the ocean and, at times the loneliness, gives rise to emotions in me tinged equally with fear and awe, and shared, I am sure, with many fishermen who have faced danger out at sea. As is typical with memory, the general daily grind of work does not surface; it is the particular and precise moments that we recall. These moments, associated with varied and strong emotions, keep memories alive. I believe there is nothing comparable to the life of the fisher folk.

The history, fascinating as it is, covers only a single aspect of our lives with Shemaron. The worry and the hours of driving up to her home in Campbeltown some three hundred miles or so from our own home in the north of England, was a challenge. The sheer amount of effort required to venture forth on such a project inevitably strained the comfortable vision of our future I once held. The minimal retirement funds we possessed had been depleted and the resulting gap filled with a large question mark, while the amount of physical labour looks like it will continue for the foreseeable future. Despite these struggles, we have brought her a long way, restoring her through a series of small undertakings. There is still much to do and at times, it feels like her future hangs on a wing and a prayer.

At some point during our time with Shemaron, a subtle bonding process – I like to call it magic – began, and I changed. It wasn't that I didn't recognise myself anymore; it was more like I recognised a new part of myself. Alone on the sea while the dawn laid claim to the day, I felt the magic, I felt my place and it was very small, an indiscernible speck on the face of time. Yet within my head, heart, and soul, the recognition of myself as that speck was immense and timeless. Until this moment I had been a happy bystander, content to indulge my husband in his vocation and to be rewarded for my efforts with the beautiful scenery that enveloped us on our road trips and the lovely nights in hotels along our way. Afterward, I was more aware of the sea and sun, of the moon and tides: how they stretched into the world and how their power might affect life the world over.

Within the boundaries where I had lived my life so far, I shifted and grew and found greater scope for adventure. These times on our boat allowed me to look at life with a different perspective. My inner eye had been opened and I could see my life as the consequence of the massive continuing ripple effect that started billions of years ago. It is easy to get lost among these ripples so I will bring the focus back to Shemaron, as she was the enabler, the catalyst, that wrought the change in me.

Whereas my husband bonded with the boat through the oil, paint, and grime, and the blood, sweat, and tears that the Shemaron experience seemed to exude, I bonded through the romance and the stories that surfaced on the wave of nostalgia that swept into Campbeltown with us when we first arrived. Mostly this nostalgia was conveyed by conversations on the harbour side, often on our deck, where sometimes a visitor would join us in the fo'c'sle for a dram in the darkening hours. We would chat below the gentle glow of the Tilley lamp until my eyelids grew heavy with boredom by countless references to engines and other mechanics, but I would be revived by the mention of the northern islands and all the adventures our companions would share.

It did take a while, but eventually my involvement came from myself and not because I was attached to Shemaron through a third party. I loved our trips out on her, I loved watching her move forward to a better state, and I loved the fact that she began to reveal her history.

Thankfully, when I looked back on our time in Campbeltown, the long hours spent on the road would fade increasingly into inconsequence in the light of our adventures. When we emerged from the car at the quayside, although we were stiff and sore, we were soothed by the scenery we had come through. It was a changing dynamic; it spun 'round us, strengthening the thread that pulled us from south to north and back again

Over the course of these car journeys, we encountered many beautiful and varied scenes. They could be made mysterious by the changing moods of the western weather; the expanse of Loch Fyne for example, could be smooth and sultry, with a colour spectrum anywhere between heather, ash, or all shades of blue. It could shine like glass and hold the hills in its embrace or it could be agitated, confused, and whipped by the wind. And then there was the sea, another changing dynamic, but on a far greater scale, which we finally reach after leaving the deep and ancient waters of West Loch Tarbert. The sea tumbled into our final miles almost touching the road. The Atlantic roll could be long and slow, it could be fast, furious, and unforgiving, ripping up the sands, or it could be gentle and welcoming, a showering of foaming kisses upon the rocks.

As we drew ever closer to our journey's end and the road eventually came to the Atlantic coast of Kintyre, the light would spill in splendour no matter the weather, falling around us to give a particular clarity to the hills, rocks, and the islands over the water. Sometimes, we could see Gigha, Islay, Jura, Ireland, and Rathlin. Sometimes, it was only the three closest islands that loomed across the sea, and at other times we could hardly make out the rocky shores of Gigha through the smoor.

Every journey was different and every time was beautiful, although in the winter when the long, black night blocked everything from view so that it felt like we were driving through endless tunnels, it was harder.

When we finally set foot on board and descended through the hatch into the lonely fo'c'sle, it seemed as though we all - Shemaron, Chris, and myself – had to adjust to each other in the confined space. Used to her long, quiet times, Shemaron seemed to recoil when we lit the stove and condensation would run and drip from the beams before she relaxed and welcomed us back. Any fresh and fragrant cosmetics, in which I may have indulged, were instantly and irrevocably overlaid with the smell of bilge, oil, and damp wood. Before we reached our compromise (Shemaron having to put up with my softer ways in return for a load of attention and the promise of a trip away from the quay), wafts of peat smoke and harbour air filtered back through the open hatches and skylights. There were no soft places to cushion my aching limbs and I walked, stooped in an exaggerated manner, for fear of thwacking my head against the oak beams.

The only comforts onboard Shemaron came from the heat of the fire, the glow from the lamp, and the gentle tilting motion as she settles continuously upon the sea. Happily, I have discovered that these few comforts are all I need; they are more valuable because of the lack of any others.

Somewhere, amid the history and the travelling and the adventure, it seemed as though we had created a different life for ourselves. We hadn't, of course, but we had added a new experience to our normal daily toil. It wasn't easy, but the lure of Kintyre, Shemaron, and the freedom that they created, beckoned us forward and northward.

Chapter 2
The Dream

Shemaron impacted our lives in very real and difficult ways – ways that we were just beginning to understand, through our dwindling finances and the physical effort of motoring half the length of the country nearly every weekend to give her the attention she required. However, the impact we experienced through happy coincidence, inspiration, history, and self-fulfilment, was beyond what money could buy.

A spark had been ignited during the 1970s in my husband's youthful years during family holidays in Kintyre, Scotland. The Malkin family spent holidays there because of a study in which their father was involved as a marine biologist. He was looking into the species and sub-species of herring and their apparent movement around the Scottish coast. I can easily understand why the family was captivated by the area. Over time, study and holiday eventually became one, allowing them to develop a love of Campbeltown and the surrounding countryside. My husband and his family returned often in subsequent years, seduced by the clear waters, hidden coves and remote beaches, to relax and rejuvenate in the easy beauty and exquisite air.

One of the holiday highlights was to race down the hill towards Campbeltown in the old Morris Oxford and arrive at the harbour in time to see the herring boats returning in the early evening. During this era, these old herring boats were probably trawling for prawns and whitefish; herring were still being caught, but they were discharged elsewhere. I have seen a similar sight myself, driving down the road to collect fish and chips to take to Shemaron for our supper as we worked on-board.

A winter's evening, the sky was patch-worked with grey as I watched a set of mizzen lights strung out across the sea winking in the swell. They were heading to Campbeltown, guided through the gloaming by the Davaar light. From the road, I could see the light clearly shining on the rocky backdrop that heralds its warning. For a brief moment, the huge rock is visible in the darkness. Davaar Island sits at the entrance to Campbeltown loch. The goats, mink, and sheep that account for the majority of the island's residents must enjoy stunning views across the sea. It was a lovely thing to watch fishing boats returning. I counted seven or eight boats, a sad little number compared to the fleets of old; the 1970s and 1980s would have seen much healthier and more numerous fishing fleets.

One gala day in 1970s Campbeltown, as the afternoon was drawing to a close but the fishing boats were still offering turns around the loch, my husband, then a young boy, secured himself a place on one of them. It was to prove a pivotal moment. The first moment he stepped onto the deck of the Boy Danny, the seed was sown, the flame ignited. Through the intervening years of births, marriages, and deaths, the memory stayed happily with him as a subtle pressure and influence in his life.

For my own part in the matter it was a much slower and more

recent transition, from mild supportive interest to a deeper and more fulfilling understanding of the people and the ring net industry. I began to recognise that certain characteristics differed between boats. For example, I knew what was meant by *carvel* or *clinker*; carvel refers to a strong frame overlaid with smooth planking, whereas clinker refers to a light frame with its strength coming from the overlapping planks. I knew that herring boats were built from oak and larch. I love the look of these ring net boats with their small wooden wheelhouses and low gunnels. I love the sheer in their decks and the cross of their masts. My own interest started growing independently from that of my husband.

I am intrigued by the fact that they were built from wood, and that this wood came from trees that grew on land, with roots that sank deep into the earth for nourishment and sustenance; this has been the way since prehistory. The idea that the wood has enabled man to travel, explore, and fish, and that it is all still happening today, although to a lesser degree is fascinating. Wood eventually became the catalyst for the power of the steam engine that enabled longer voyages and larger vessels. I am enlivened by the natural elements that surround the whole idea of fishing and I love hearing the stories that live on in the memories of people we have met, some of which I hope to share during the course of this book.

I hijacked my husband's dream, unwittingly of course. I have been carried on his passion, and involved in his evolving acquisition of knowledge. I have fretted through his dilemmas and in the beginning I watched from the sidelines, while he followed his heart and instinct through the doorway that led us to a beautiful and adventurous new world. In 2008, the dream of owning an old fishing boat was finally realised. We have since then also realised the level of commitment and expense involved in acquiring it; happily this is balanced by the adventure and romance it brings to our lives. Part of the dream was to write a book, and this is the part of his dream that I have hijacked, though I think he is happy with the prospect. I will rely on his propensity for exacting detail and he must allow for my tendency towards the romantic.

The seed sown during childhood was sprouting, nurtured by increasing experience and knowledge. Over the subsequent years, Chris became more and more involved with the historical record of fishing. He made trips to the Scottish Fisheries Museum in Anstruther and returned many times to reacquaint himself with the fishing communities along the East Coast. He would collect small scraps of information, which grew into a detailed record of the ring net industry. Recognising the importance of these traditional boats as the last of their kind, because they had become less suited to modern fishing methods, and fearing that at any given moment they might disappear forever, inspired a sense of urgency in him. As he grew older, the passion to try and save one of these beautiful ring netters that were likely to vanish grew stronger, but there seemed no way forward. Feeling powerless and frustrated by his need and inability to act, he had to be content to stand back watching and waiting.

In 2004, we visited the fishing village of Maidens, on the Ayrshire coast, it is an important harbour in our tale, and a place to which I will return more often as our story shifts westward. There was an old ring net boat submerged in Maidens harbour; it lay as though someone had just finished a day's fishing, left her, and never returned, a forlorn wreck washed with the tide. Blue paint still coated her flanks where she sat in the silt. A tattered remnant of Ayrshire heritage, about to fall from recent historic record through the black hole that grows a little each time a fisherman passes on, leaving in his wake a broken industry.

Standing by the sea, we fancifully wondered if this boat might indeed be one of the famous boats owned by the Sloan brothers; of course it wasn't, it was the Caberfeidh (a Gaelic name meaning "horns of the stag")

I think there are varying degrees of the past: the ancient past, the historical past, and the recent past, all of which reach out to us during different times and at different places. It was the recent past that called out to us then, and we wanted to know more about this boat. It lay weighed down by the silt thickening in the undisturbed water, but our thoughts and the history could not connect at that time and they missed each other in the wind. Like the moon on the tide, the pull of the dream was getting stronger. However, there were a few other circumstances that needed to connect before man and boat would come together.

Life moves inevitably onwards, taking us to unknown destinations. Chris and I had one or two weekends away on our motorbike, which centred more and more often on Tarbert and Kintyre. Sitting in the pillion position – behind my husband on the bike, the world rushed by on a haze of buffeting and wind noise. Particular things would make an impression on me, enhanced by the gush of elements and the clarity of the scenery in the split seconds of passage. I remember the smell of the hedgerows, the wayside flowers and herbs, blooming in pockets as we burst from one moment to the next. A stag, its great rack of antlers lost in the grass, as it lowered its head to drink, the sun on the lochs, the colour of the sea, seals like stone, noses and tails to the sun.

On one of our rides we visited Carradale, a small village north of Campbeltown. We were searching, as always, for the boats that lived in historic memory. An old wooden trawler was tied up against the pier; it was more delicately and smoothly proportioned than almost all other boats around and obviously still working. The name painted along her gunnels and across her wheelhouse was Shemaron and she rested comfortably, now and then gently pulling on her ropes. Later that day, we discovered that Shemaron was formerly known as Wistaria and was the very same boat we had read accounts of, belonging to the Sloan family. She was alive and well in Carradale!

Matt and Billy Sloan came from a family of successful fishermen; during the Second World War they were both officers in the Navy. They had a reputation for catching herring that was second to none. During the 50s and 60s using the boats Veronica, Virginia, Wistaria, Watchful and Bairns Pride they were consistently successful with the ring net. Their attention to detail in every aspect of the boat and gear, their keen eye for business, their instincts and skill at finding herring combined to ensure they were very influential in fishing communities around Scotland.

It became our habit to seek out Shemaron each time we were in the area. There was always a day in which we managed to make time for the boat, though for my own part these times were not yet inspired by my own interest but were a way sharing time with my husband.

Our family by now had developed a deep love affair with Argyll, or more precisely, with a little cottage on the shores of Loch Caolisport. We enjoyed times of easy adventure. Down the road that led to nowhere and in the land that time forgot, we would unwind. Even as the children grew each year, they always loved to return. We could swim from the cottage doorway, clamber over the rocks, or explore the estate. We would pick our way through the woods and ferns that towered in Jurassic fashion over our heads, and make our way to deserted, white, sandy beaches that lay just on the tree line, or just over the hill. Once there, we would sunbathe with the seals and swim quickly hoping they wouldn't come too close. At night, we would take refuge from the midges within whitewashed walls and sit by the large picture window that looked out to the open sea. The darkness would come down so softly, but eventually everything would be so black that nothing could be seen, except sometimes the lights of a fishing boat crossing the head of the loch. They were such simple holidays and I was often left wondering how I would cope at home for another year until we could come back. From a mother's point of view, it was so lovely to have uninterrupted time during which my family could be together, away from the personal pressures that inevitably invaded our daily routines. I looked forward to these holidays so much, always ready for the healing they brought.

It takes more than passion alone to bring about a dream; the magic that had entered our hearts had been weaving together other events in our lives. We run our own business and had at that time been thinking about expansion. To this end we had in place a bank loan with an agreeably low interest rate. Our business circumstance then changed, and finding ourselves with no need of the loan, we intended to cancel the arrangement.

Chris went down to Tarbert one day during our holiday to see Shemaron; we always knew we could find her on the quay. She had been sold and was no longer a working boat. While he was standing opposite her, regretting her languishing state, his mobile phone rang; it happened to be the bank, enquiring into our status concerning the arranged loan.

How often in life do we stand literally facing our dreams with money readily available to bring them to fruition? Back in Newcastle the next day, a brief telephone conversation confirmed that Shemaron was owned in three parts and one of the shares was for sale. We expressed an interest, now one hundred per cent sure that we would at long last have an opportunity to own at least part of an old fishing boat.

During the pre-sale conversations back at home, we learned that there was some doubt about the engine because it had a loud top end noise, and that various options were being considered as to the best course of action. Our financial interest in Shemaron at this time probably helped to alleviate some pressure among the shareholders; however, it also forced the issue concerning the cost of the engine repair. We were therefore able to purchase our share, at a reasonable sum.

There were of course many more telephone conversations concerning money and the amounts needed to restore an old ring net boat. The engine was the biggest obstacle; a boat with no engine loses its purpose. I imagine this was a point in the proceedings where dreams had come face to face with reality, a problem had been acknowledged but the possible cost of setting it right was always just out of reach. It became apparent that the two remaining shareholders were grasping at the eroded remnants of their own dreams. After further negotiation, a figure was agreed upon for the purchase of their shares. It was by now 2008 and we had at last become the full owners of Shemaron. We stood back, teetering a little from the consequences of our actions, blissfully happy.

Of course, we returned to Tarbert as soon as possible to feel the inspiration of our lives literally beneath our feet and explore our boat. And as we stood in the damp confines of the fish hold, our exhilaration spent, other emotions began to surface as we realised the enormity of the restoration task.

Shemaron

Salty sad and peeling planks
Blind glass in a lazy frame
Still strong in wind and rain.
Sound deck, dry and quiet now,
Echoes of sea and surf and scale.
Declining carvel crusted bow
Lapped by gentle waters soft and slight.
Stripped of rigs and ropes and winching steel,
Scrappy colours losing hold.
No lights to swing on shantied waves
No nets dumped damp on deck.

Chapter 3
Realising the Dream

Pushing our fears aside, we began work in earnest and many hours were spent on the road between Newcastle and Tarbert. We got in touch with a former skipper of Shemaron who seemed pleased that something positive was going to happen with his old boat. Chris had spent some time working with two smaller fishing boats on Tyneside, so maybe this lent us some credibility; at this point we had no idea how things were going to work out. We arranged to meet with a marine engineer on Shemaron in early autumn, with the intent of making a serious attempt at the renovation.

There was a maze of wires, seacocks, and pumps that somehow connected in crucial sequences and enabled the engine to run. Comfortable with my husband's capabilities in his new project, I was supremely un-worried. Below decks, water was up to the gearbox, the inside was dripping with condensation and it took three or four hours to fully pump her out. I took it all in my stride imagining lots of hot sunny afternoons on deck. Chris, on the other hand, was beginning to feel levels of stress that were to prove a recurring part of the bittersweet experience of renovating an old boat.

The engineer charged the batteries and the engine started. It ran evenly but there was a loud tapping noise coming from the top end. Various fuel pipes were disconnected and we discovered that the engine was only running on four out of its six cylinders. The tapping noise came and went and as we listened, it suddenly stopped. Unfortunately, the noise came back but worse than ever.

The engineer quickly reached for the switch to turn off the engine, saying, "Sorry, Chris, it's finished." I still didn't appreciate the task ahead. So far Shemaron had behaved exactly as I expected an old boat to behave.

Before we became involved with Shemaron, rainwater had entered the cylinders of the engine via the exhaust. Water is incompressible and when an attempt was made to start the engine the resulting hydraulic lock caused serious damage to the bearings and crankshaft. We had seen old photographs of Shemaron laid up with a bucket placed over the exhaust, precisely to prevent this occurrence.

The engineer stayed with us and we employed him to rebuild the engine. He subsequently employed a mate who assisted in preparing the hull for painting. At this time, our work commitments in Newcastle prevented us from making the journey to Tarbert and we had to content ourselves with regular progress updates.

The engine rebuild continued slowly. We were sourcing parts from different places. Some parts were new, some reconditioned, and some second-hand. Jobs like this tend to grow. Perhaps the crankshaft and connecting rods need to be replaced – then surely the pistons and liners also need replacing, and if the pistons and liners are replaced, then why not the camshaft and followers? Chris tells me he can still hear voices in his head saying, *"The job's going well, Chris, but you might want to consider,"* or *"Have you thought of…?"* These phone calls usually ended with some outlay for an expensive part such as an alternator, fuel pump, or starter motor.

The engine we were working on replaced a second-hand Caterpillar engine that was installed in the early 1980s, which had replaced the original Kelvin KR6. Eventually a text message arrived, marking the moment the engine started for the first time. The text included a sound recording and Chris used this for some time as the ring tone on his phone, much to the extreme irritation of everyone we knew!

The engineer's mate continued with the painting preparations, stripping the hull back to bare wood. We had decided on a mid-blue colour, but he mixed a slightly different shade; he had a knack for knowing how things would look when they were finished. For six months, we hadn't managed to get up to Tarbert very often, and when we returned in March 2009 and saw the boat newly painted, we thought she looked perfect. That Easter our teenage daughters came aboard for our first voyage. Wrapped in layers of blankets and huddled together on the fish hold hatch, they were seriously un-impressed but united in their lacklustre support for our boating venture. Our engineer was also on board. He had become a good friend, and was there to monitor all the vital pressures and temperatures of the newly rebuilt Caterpillar 3306 engine.

I sat on deck with the girls and enjoyed the trip, but the moment was really for my husband. Nothing could spoil the magnitude and thrill of those special first moments on the sea when he took Shemaron out of the harbour for the first time. The feel of the 55 foot hull riding the swell became indelibly printed on his mind. He had taken the first step in the long journey of learning how to handle Shemaron.

Later on that same weekend, she was dried out behind the fish quay in Tarbert, so the hull, rudder, and propeller could be checked. As far as we could tell there seemed to be no major problems. We made the journey to Tarbert several times over the next several weeks and began to make Shemaron habitable. Whilst undergoing the repairs, the engine had been hauled forward and suspended in the fish hold, a situation which added to the gunk and grunge that had built up over time. There was a lot of cleaning to do!

That summer we spent a few weekends at Portavadie and had a couple of trips to Otter Ferry. We also took Shemaron to the Crinan boat festival. She was not really ready but we thought it would be good fun to go through the canal. As the year of 2009 progressed, more work was completed on our boat – hundreds of little jobs and several more complex ones. Chris was getting to know her better and was slowly becoming aware of how big this project was. We used her for a few weekends and enjoyed getting to know the sea around Tarbert and Arran.

In September, we decided to take Shemaron out of the water to work on the hull. East Rothesay dock in Glasgow seemed like a good place, it wasn't too expensive, and we could work on her ourselves rather than use a boat yard's work force. The engineer's mate was going to spend much of his time painting and overseeing things when we couldn't be there. We planned to use specialists for other tasks as needed. It took a while to gather the larch, fastenings, and paint, but by late October the boat was ready to leave.

A broken fuel pump primer and the resultant flat batteries threatened to delay the departure, but they were swiftly dealt with and Shemaron left for Clydebank. The route took her through the Kyles of Bute, up the river Clyde, under the Erskine Bridge, and into the heart of the ex-shipbuilding area of Clydebank. I have always thought ex-industrial areas have a powerful and sombre feel; at dusk on a grey winter day the melancholy hung heavy in the air. Winter had not quite arrived, but its shadow was brooding over Clydebank that evening. Shemaron was secured in the dock alongside two other boats. The boats seemed to be waiting for something. They had an air about them that hovered between expectancy and hopeless acceptance. Shemaron was left looking small and forlorn. We had arranged for Shemaron to be lifted out of the water the next day but we had to return to work in Newcastle. Chris was able to return a few days later to see how things were getting on.

The first time I saw Shemaron out of the water in Clydebank it was a winter's evening. She stood tall under the glow of a street lamp and there was a thin covering of snow on the ground. It was a still night and rows of hulls stretched away, buried in the unaccustomed darkness. When we returned the next day the wind was up, tarpaulins flapped over frustrated boats, and I felt the first tiny pricks of concern that Shemaron might come to harm in the unhealthy frigid conditions. My memories of this time are cold and harsh.

Another bleak, cold day when we returned to look over Shemaron, we discovered that ice had split a water pipe. The winter was proving to be extremely cold and we were facing problems we hadn't prepared for. Normally salt water does not freeze, but the brackish water from the Clyde had got into the cooling system and frozen easily. We knew the nails had to be replaced though we had no idea how manage this, and the propeller and rudder we had sent away to be refurbished still weren't back.

We felt unprepared and under-funded for the challenge ahead. A challenge can perhaps be something to rise to, it is exhilarating to be on the successful side, but for every winner there must be a loser. To be caught up in a challenge that is spiralling into financial chaos is a desperate place to be.

We tested the loose planks with a hammer; a sharp retort meant healthy and secure planks, a dull retort meant loose planks and rusty nails. We were getting quite a few dull retorts. We had conflicting advice concerning our next course of action and some terrifying quotes. We decided to get someone who could properly survey the hull. About 70% of the nails below the water line needed replacing. A talented boat builder was employed to complete the job and what could have taken weeks to accomplish was completed in one. Our fears and panic subsided under skilled and experienced hands.

It seems appropriate to talk about our friend, the engineer's mate, at this point. As anyone who knew him was aware, he had battled for years with alcohol addiction. When we met him he had been dry for eighteen months. While he was in Clydebank, for some reason he started drinking again. We met him one Sunday morning and he told us he had drunk ten pints and some vodka the night before. He bitterly regretted it. We were concerned about the situation, and sure enough, the next day we got a call from the boat yard owner saying that he was worried. He felt that our friend would be putting himself and the boat yard at risk yard if he stayed overnight. The level of kindness the owner of the yard and his staff showed in dealing with this situation stays with us. A lot of trouble was caused by this state of affairs, yet the yard was very concerned for the well-being of this man. Our engineer who was working in Stranraer at the time, dropped everything and drove the three hours to Glasgow so he could collect our friend and take him home.

In the grim boat yard winter the small work force we had assembled laboured through the cold days, gradually bringing Shemaron to a more sprightly state of well-being. We had employed the skills of a talented sign writer, who, realised that not being paid and also being responsible for an unfinished job, would only make things worse for our alcoholic friend. His offer to take on extra work without charge thereby ensuring our troubled friend didn't suffer a cut in wages touched our hearts. In the event our friend was able to manage his addiction, he came back to work and finished his job. The reaction of these people to the problem at hand showed a level of care and understanding that we had not encountered before. We developed a great respect for everyone involved.

As the days of spring 2010 got warmer, so did our mood. A huge effort was being put into Shemaron and around Easter, we were able to re-launch her.

Short, wintry days are good for wooden boats; Shemaron was no exception. Generally weather conditions during the winter months keep a boat damp, the wood remains moist and the planks fit together tightly. During the summer, warm winds and long hours of sunshine have a drying effect on the wood causing it to shrink; gaps can sometimes appear in the planking. When we lowered Shemaron back into the water she remained tight and floated without taking in water. Free from other commitments, during the spring of 2010, we were able to take advantage of a break in the weather and set off down the Clyde to take her home for a little rest and recuperation.

Chapter 4
Getting Out On the Water

It was a relief to have Shemaron back in the water. She was proving to be a strong boat. When I saw her out of the water in Clydebank I thought she looked a little ill at ease in the unnatural surroundings; however, her stance was strong. Her situation was hard and although delicate, it was controlled. She was being cared for.

I had seen other ring net boats, the Wellspring and Oak Lea, out of the water, and they had always fascinated me. Even in their dilapidated states they held a poise and beauty. There was a gracefulness about them that was returning to the land; like they were a gift, well used and appreciated but their life cycle had ended too soon. They were dissolving around the roots from whence they came in the very beginning.

I was drawn to the incongruity of the situation of these ruined boats when they were out of their natural habitat. They were no longer whole; they were hauled up on the shore, their strong beautiful bows towered above me but ached in their decay. Their sterns stood gallantly but their bodies were broken. They waited out their ends of days so close to the sea on which they had flexed their muscles in times gone by. If the water ever touched them now, it would drag away with it some fragile, frail, and failing part. In comparison, Shemaron had stood firm. She had a solid and substantial presence and seemed eager to get back into the water.

We steamed away from the city, leaving behind the industrial riversides that have changed so much during the span of Shemaron's life. For the most part we found ourselves alone in the breadth of the river pushing through the ghosts of yesteryear. It was an odd thing; the boat yard, although uncomfortable, had other wooden boats and small crafts for company but out on the river we felt a strange loneliness. We steamed steadily, slowly making our way to the sea. Shemaron was happy to be back in the water, I could feel it.

The whole experience was an education that didn't correspond with my normal way of life. It seems peculiar when I remember how different I felt aboard Shemaron then, compared to now. It was an intrusion; although I had invited myself into the situation, Shemaron had no choice in the matter. Oblivious to her passengers she carried me, but I felt like I scratched along the surface of a painting. I was there but not part of the picture.

By the time we reached the river mouth, I was starting to lose sensation in my toes. As we approached the Kyles of Bute I realised no amount of tea, Tunnocks Tea Cakes, or soup was going to keep me warm. My feet were like solid blocks of ice and the cold was seeping slowly but surely into my body. I gave up the deck and went down into the fo'c'sle to get warm. The stove was alight and I sat for a long time while it chased the cold from my bones. Below deck the engine was loud; it was an unexpectedly comforting sound. Arran was just visible in the distance when I climbed back out of the hatch the island of Bute was on my left and the Cowal Peninsula on my right. The heaviness in the air was lifting and we passed Skate Island in sunshine. Looking towards Kintyre, it could have been a quiet summer afternoon. It was only another couple of hours or so to Tarbert. Shemaron would soon be home.

I remember the sense of release and relief! We had done it; Shemaron was safe, secure, re-nailed, and smartened up. It had been a couple of days full of cold and sharp edges. I think that was when things started to change in my attitude towards our boat. We had successfully concluded our task; there had even been parts of the undertaking that I had actually enjoyed – in a "scratching along the surface" sort of way. A tiny chink had appeared in the easy suburban husk that encased my life.

The purchase of Shemaron indulged Chris's sense of adventure. His steadfast resolution not to become bogged down with the mundane or the banal aspects of life has at times proved exceptionally difficult to deal with. At the same time however, it is exactly this quality that soothes my own fears that life might begin to rotate in a meaningless direction, and nurtures my own sense of adventure.

In the months that followed, more major work was undertaken on Shemaron. The forecastle had a double skin, maybe for warmth and neatness; the area between the two layers was the only part of Shemaron we hadn't seen properly. We drilled holes and put cameras through to check if everything was all right. Some parts were very wet with rainwater. Seawater kind of pickles the wood and helps preserve it, but rainwater has the opposite effect and has been the ruin of many good boats. Although it was very wet, we found little rot, we added better ventilation and treated the wood with various chemicals. At the same time, the fish hold combings were replaced, as close as possible to the original design. Countless other jobs were undertaken and completed.

As the summer of 2010 progressed we became more relaxed and we started to break our chores on board with short trips around the locality. I think the owners of the local hardware store must have clapped their hands in glee whenever we ventured through the door! There was so much painting to do and cleaning to get on top of. We must have spent a small fortune on polishes, cloths, buckets, solvents, paints, peat, coal, kindling, and firelighters, not to mention eating and cooking accoutrements.

On one of these trips we steamed up to Inverary near the head of Loch Fyne. We became part of the view we had admired so often from the car window. The scenery didn't just waft past us, it flowed around us; we breathed it, tasted it; it spoke to us and demanded our interaction. The colour spectrum I described previously as heather, ash, and all shades of blue, subtly merged from one colour to another. The colours had become part of the progression of the day, not a snapshot glimpsed as we bolted by on the road.

When we arrived at Inverary, we tied up against the beautiful but dilapidated old steamer pier in the company of Vital Spark and Arctic Penguin. There was no ladder up to the quay and although we managed to get on shore by utilising a ladder that we kept on board, once was enough for me, and I was marooned on board for most of the time. Chris ventured up and down more easily, returning once with a donation of scones and cakes that the tearoom on Arctic Penguin had not managed to sell. Later under the gentle glowing light from the paraffin lamp we enjoyed this welcome supplement to our rations.

We left the next day in a fine Scottish mist, carefully picking out our route using charts but relying predominantly on the plotter. Most of the time I kept my eyes peeled for unexpected things looming out of the fog, and when I took the wheel for a short time I was dismayed at how quickly we veered off course. With no landmarks in sight, it was a remarkably different experience steering a boat through the mist, compared to our colourful voyage on the previous day. Thankfully, in keeping with its natural Scottish character, the weather changed within a couple of hours and we saw our route ahead clearly.

Sometimes we would stay at our berth on the pontoon in Tarbert and work on board. If it was a pleasant evening we might take the short hop round the bay and pick up a mooring by Stonefield Castle. One particular night there was a full moon. Away from the bright city lights, the world turned in shades of grey, and the loch ran silver about our feet. There was a wonderful clarity in the moonlight. We sometimes went ashore to the hotel for dinner. It was not the most elegant manoeuvre, alighting from a 55 foot fishing boat into a rubber dingy, and boarding again was even worse, but the food was good. I did wonder if it was all worth it when I lost my footing and found myself hanging from the gunnels!

The old steamer pier at Tighnabruaich became a favourite destination. The paddle steamer Waverly calls there. Once or twice we had to stand off while its passengers embarked and disembarked. We would settle in for the night nestled by the side of the pier while anglers cast their fishing lines over our heads. They eventually idled away in the dusk and we would be left alone. It would become very quiet on the white Victorian pier. Our little fire would be stoked up for the night and we would cook our evening meal on the two ring camping stove. We ate sitting on deck wrapped in blankets, as the gloaming settled around us. The chatter of gulls and oystercatchers quieted and sometimes we heard the raucous cry of a heron carried over the Kyles. When I look back, it seems as though these times were part of a gentle initiation, a soft shift into comfortable adventure.

Another place we grew very fond of was Portavadie Marina; it was only a few minutes across the water from Tarbert. It was a tranquil and serene place. There was always plenty of room on the pontoons so securing ourselves was an easy task, we always felt relaxed. Ever eager to explore, remember, and experience everything around me in the vast outside, on the sea or otherwise, I persuaded Chris to walk with me up into the hills. It was a soft damp day. We climbed swiftly up from the marina and very soon Shemaron looked small. Up on the top we rested a minute to catch our breath and take in the new landscape. It was rough moorland patch-worked with woods; off to the east, maybe two or three miles distant a valley opened to the sea. Where the land broke and the sea and sky met, something was hovering in the air; at first we thought it was a hang glider but as it came closer we realised it was an eagle.

There is the natural world and then there is the world that we have created within that world, the world of streets, buildings, and industry. Seeing the Golden Eagle was like being out on the sea. I was outside my world, suddenly at the pinnacle of the ultimate wild, a witness to the greater picture. Without any perceptible movement of its wings, the eagle came towards us, its minuscule movements sifting the air currents, it had ultimate control. From the horizon with wings outstretched and without a flap or a flutter, it covered the distance from the sea to the moorland where we stood in the time it took to take a breath. It disappeared at times, made invisible by the bark and the bracken, embraced by the hillsides and woodland as it hunted under the low cloud. At certain angles it would appear as a thin dark line in the sky, a master of stealth, speed, and camouflage. I saw its talons held rigid as it flew and its hooked beak as it hovered, soared and dived above us. I wondered what I would see if I could look into its eye, what wild and ancient calling would radiate from its pupil if our worlds collided. I tore myself away eventually, leaving the beautiful, amazing bird to the tawny hillsides and spinning vistas of land and sea.

At Portavadie, our days were punctuated with bouts of lazy industry. We were coating the newly constructed fish hold combing with boiled linseed oil, every now and again stopping to sit or sleep in the sun for a few minutes. It was a gentle time. One night, we sat and watched a meteor shower. We were far enough away from all other boats to feel happily disconnected and sat on deck wrapped in the woolly quietude of the night. All time was thrown open above us; the past, the present, and the future, were unfolding on the astral plains. We were the smallest speck on the particular meridian that locked us in time and space. All our horizons fell in stars and splendour or climbed in vertical wonder. We called to each other each time we saw a trailing light, each falling star a trickle of luck – we did not yet know how much we would need. Our bows streamed with starlight; we were suspended in our globe, with the firmament above. The ocean below was catching the stars and rocking them gently in its salty caress, always spinning softly towards the dawn.

Exceptional moments continue to rise vividly in my memory. On an early trip to Campbeltown, it was hot and sunny with no wind, a picture postcard afternoon. We were just off the coast of Arran. The sea was so still the mountain reflections seemed to sleep on the surface of the water. I was on deck watching the bow ripples break up the colours on the polished surface as we moved gently along. They kaleidoscoped into patterns of blue and grey, running away and settling behind us on the windless sound. On our return up the Kilbrannan Sound, we saw a basking shark. We watched as its huge body meandered through the water. Basking sharks have been around for millions of years, a living link to prehistoric times. Thousands of millennia fell away as we watched this creature weave past our bow.

The thought has come to me often whilst spending time on the west coast of Scotland, that maybe things have not changed so much. In some odd places, perhaps things have hardly changed at all since the early inhabitants first settled on the land. The sea has changed even less; it still holds many secrets. I am aware of the wildness of the place and of the influence the tide has on the culture that has developed in this region.

I read a passage from a book written by a man who had journeyed around the coast in his canoe – I think he slipped into this wildness for a time, beaching his canoe and resting; waking to take advantage of the tides and continue his journey; living with the pulse of nature. I see this with the creatures when I watch the wildlife in the area. Otters and birds feed on the margins between land and sea; they hunt on the rocks and in the shallows exposed by receding tides. I have always wanted to live by natural rules. I have secretly abhorred the daily humdrum of the working day. I think this is one of the reasons why I have enjoyed being on Shemaron so much.

We were living the dream, living a story which could easily be called, "Never Ending Journey", "When Worlds Collide", or countless other enthralling enticements of adventure daring and enlightenment. We were lost in tide time, happy to be within a circle of our own making and within a time of our own taking.

Chapter 5
Campbeltown

It had taken three years, but by 2011 I was beginning to associate my time on board Shemaron with beauty and happiness. I can't say that my interest was keen, but it was there. Shemaron seemed a little more at ease in my presence; there was a mutual contemplation between us.

Chris was absorbed with the next task in the renovation: employing the skills of a local craftsman to fashion the masts and other rigging. Plans to assemble the rigging coincided happily with the discovery of a scaled drawing of a 1930s ring netter. The drawing was found in a skip by the man whose services we had secured to help us with the task; it was a remarkable coincidence and we took it as a good omen. It showed in detail the way in which the rigging was arranged. The main mast, mizzenmast, and boom were crafted and carefully assembled. We had been given the brailer pole from the Irma, a pre-war Carradale ring net boat, and this was fitted at the same time.

The assembly of the rigging had a two-fold effect; on the one hand it brought Shemaron back to her former glory; on the other, it marked the end of our "easy money" because the last of the loan money had been spent. The original amount of £40,000 had covered the purchase of the boat plus all the major expenses so far. When we had needed money to pay for re-conditioning the engine, Shemaron's time in Clydebank, and the other initial costs of our project it had been readily available. In retrospect, this was an important turning point in the story. Future funding for our project would have to be found, whilst simultaneously paying off the loan. I did not appreciate the extent of maintenance Shemaron would require and with so much of the important work completed, I continued looking forward in blissful ignorance.

A year had gone by since the last boat festival at Crinan and we were looking forward to going again. During the weeks running up to this highlight of the summer, the rigging had been completed and arranged in the iconic way of the West Coast herring fleets with the crossed masts. We arrived in Tarbert late one summer evening to find Shemaron freshly painted for the occasion. This lovely gesture was a last minute surprise. The paint was not quite dry as we clambered on board, but she looked fantastic. It was always hard arriving at the boat at night after the long drive, but it didn't take long to settle in, and sleep came easily.

Shemaron looked so lovely enhanced by the yellow glow from the recently constructed rigging. She obviously enjoyed the reconnection to her former life as Wistaria. I felt as though she had found her signature. Her life had run a full circle; she was getting ready to tell her story.

We rose early the next morning to get a good start. It was going to be a long day travelling through the Crinan Canal. Shemaron's ex-skipper, Sandy Galbraith, joined us. Whenever Sandy came along it was a relaxed trip; we were always reassured by his presence. We made our way up Loch Fyne; it was a warm morning even though it was still early. Not long into our journey, we saw our second basking shark, its tail and dorsal fin threading slowly up the loch. Although this was the second time we had seen one of these great fish, it was no less awe-inspiring.

We had to wait at Ardrishaig while the lock gate opened. Small boats were tied up all around the sides of the basin and it was with the practiced ease of a seasoned mariner that Sandy brought Shemaron to rest alongside one of these boats. He picked a particular spot to rest that kept Shemaron clear of the buffeting water that fell into the basin as the water levels equalised. We were sitting beside a quiet little boat, our bow towered above it, with the engine chugging satisfactorily in neutral while we waited. Some moments later a rather disgruntled boat occupant was straining to glare up at us. As an innocent bystander, I happily left it to Sandy to explain why he had found it necessary to rest Shemaron so close to the sleeping boat. A few moments later we picked up another couple of passengers and regaled them with the tale of the disgruntled man and Sandy's cool handling of the situation. A withering comment about the sort of man, who is still in his pyjamas so late in the day, was the shrugged response from Sandy!

We slipped effortlessly into the leafy overhangs of the canal and I went to prepare breakfast in the fo'c'sle: cheese scones warmed on the stove. We ate as we flowed sedately through the tree-lined confines and straight stretched edges. In some places, growth was so dense that branches almost touched our flanks as we moved languorously over the silty course. The stove gave off a peaty aroma, which hung in our wake, a testament to our passage. We made fairly good time to Cairnbaan where we had to wait in a queue – this was pretty much the order of the day from then on. Lots of boats were making their way to the festival; it was slow going through the fifteen locks.

We left the crowded vegetation behind and were waiting in a more open part of the canal. Nearby, the Iron Age Dunadd sat high at the head of the marshy glen where it once ruled over the Scottish kingdom of Dalriada. It is a most engaging place, and the spot where the ancient kings of Dalriada were crowned. I have visited the Dunn on foot, set my boot to its pagan track and climbed through the tumbled stones. From the top, the view is spectacular and there is a carving of a footprint in the stone. It is said that when kings of Scotland were inaugurated, they placed one foot in this carving, a symbolic action during a ceremony that bound them to the land.

From the top of the Dun I could see everything, a natural awe radiated out and resounded back from the hills and the islands across the sea. It was easy to imagine how the ancient rulers might have felt connected to the land in such a place. From the deck of Shemaron, I got a different perspective. Being on the water gave me a richer understanding; it brought history to life. If the years could be rewound, the river would still run, the sea would still roll off the marsh, and boats would still be navigating these western waterways. The ancient moss would be receiving treasures, holding secrets, and bearing the meandering Add to the Atlantic. In the present day the Moine Mhor (this is a Gaelic phrase, Moine meaning peat moss or bog, and Mhor meaning full or large; hence "The Great Moss") holds its place among the veils, settled in the mists that cloud the boundaries between life and death, and to me has a sacred feel about it.

The marsh holds much that is unknown, echoes of other times, whereas the stone circles, monoliths, and carvings that cover the landscape around this place are solid monuments, direct messages from the past. Rocks were carved because of their permanence, notes from our ancestors that we cannot interpret, bold statements resolute through the ages. We passed near the remains of the old oak woods, which were cleared by early farmers when they settled the land. Before the oaks, the land was covered with birch, ash, and hazel. It was seeded on the wind after the retreat of the ice.

We continued slowly along the canal. Shemaron quickened in the familiar landscape, and there was the softest voice, so fragile that I almost missed it, as if she whispered, "I have been here before." The sound of it was lost in the rotation of her propeller; I caught it as it fell. It brushed my senses but I couldn't hold it. I lost it in the brilliance of the day. I like to think she was beginning to recognise her liminal state: she stood on the one hand in the past and on the other quite firmly in the present.

Wistaria Crinan canal late 1950s-early 1960s (H. McPhee)

Wistaria, west-east Crinan canal, late 1950's-early1960s (H. McPhee)

In some places, the canal was so narrow we could comfortably pass the time of day with passers-by. At one point, we ran aground and had to push ourselves off a mud bank. At last, we entered the packed Crinan Basin. In a cacophony of engine noise and smoke, we slowly manoeuvred Shemaron into her berth. Slumbering skippers roused in consternation as our old trawler skimmed by the bows of their expensive, classic yachts.

The three of us were however at odds with the jolly atmosphere in the basin. Shemaron was re-connecting with her former self; she had been a hardworking boat and the festival frivolity didn't sit well with her serious nature. I was eager for the next stage of our journey to begin and Chris was also looking forward to the open space beyond the lock gates.

It had been a long but satisfying day. The evening was still and it was hard to imagine that the weather could be any better. During her former life in the working world of ring net boats, Shemaron, then known as Wistaria, had once arrived at the Crinan basin on her way home from the Minch. The evening then was anything but still, the wind was up and the sea was rolling so hard that the lock gates could not be opened. Wistaria had to bear the onslaught of the storm and seek a safe harbour elsewhere. Safe harbours in this part of the world are few and far between especially in a storm, it would have taken some hours before she was comfortable again. It is a shame our boat cannot tell us how the crew felt at that moment, when they had been no doubt anticipating the calm safety of the basin. There were hard situations to deal with as a fisherman.

The next day dawned bright and fine. We sat in the sunshine most of the morning while gorgeous old yachts tied against us, waiting to go through the sea lock. At last it was our turn; the basin had emptied nicely, making it easier for us to move around. A little feather of anticipation fluttered in my stomach as we inched towards the lock gates. So far our times on board Shemaron had been spent in the sheltered waters of the Clyde. Having no need to get ourselves back home and with the good weather forecast holding, we had decided not to return through the canal but to venture onto the open sea.

We began to fall slowly between the brick lined walls, and the flutter in my stomach turned to a feeling of excitement. Eventually, with the lock towering above us, the gate opened and we moved out into the Sound of Jura – the ocean proper. It was an amazing feeling, to emerge from the close quarters of the lock into the wide blue yonder. It was a deep moment, a moment of clarity and culmination; it expanded around us before settling like a cloak on our shoulders. It was a dream come true for Chris. For me, it was incredible. My limited experience had broadened literally to the horizons on the Atlantic. I stood at the bow as we edged into the sea, having my Titanic moment. We could have gone anywhere, the Hebrides and beyond, Colonsay, or Ireland. We were free, it was an adventure and it was another beginning.

As I stood on the foredeck thrilling with the experience, Chris thankfully was in control at the wheel, already plotting our course. My bubbles of excitement settled to a thrum of exhilaration. We decided to head for Islay. We bent to our course. The sea was calm, the hours drifted by, and I tried to imagine how it might have been for Shemaron on different days in different times.

It reminded me of a time we had heard a recollection from a fisherman who used to be at the herring. As a young boy watching from the school window in Mallaig one stormy day, he recalled seeing two ring net boats, the Bairns Pride and our boat, then named Wistaria, coming in to the harbour to discharge their catches. They had been fishing round the Outer Hebrides; because of the wild weather conditions, they were the only boats around. They each discharged 90 cran of herring and turned back straight away, into the gales on the Sound of Sleat. In this story, I pictured Wistaria standing on end in the teeth of the westerly wind. I was happy that the weather conditions were forecast to remain calm for our first voyage. We steamed by the top of Loch Caolisport and I wondered if anyone was staying in the little white cottage where we spent so many lovely holidays, and if they were, I wondered if they might pick us out as we steamed by.

Herring were caught here on occasion. I came across an account of Oak Lea fishing here in Tommy Ralston's book, Captains and Commanders. One night, years ago, the ring net boat Oak Lea set out from Tarbert through the Crinan canal, shot her net in Loch Caolisport, filled her hold with herring and returned. (See chart on page) It seems to have been part of a gentle subterfuge for ring net boats to keep a little mystery around their intended "hunting grounds," especially if they were enjoying success. Later that same night, Oak Lea returned to the favourable loch via the Mull of Kintyre. When she arrived she found the rest of the herring fleet at anchor, having searched the area to no avail. Oak Lea had put out her lights to remain undetected, and so she slipped quietly by and headed towards the inner loch. She shot her net again, and again, caught enough herring to fill her hold plus the hold of her neighbouring boat.

We continually monitored our time and position while the day wore on. We made good progress. We decided to press on towards Gigha. We knew we needed an early start the next morning to catch the tides correctly around the Mull of Kintyre, and Gigha was nearer to our destination. Gigha is a small island off the western coast of Kintyre; it has been inhabited since prehistoric times and boasts long hours of sunshine and a mild climate – a perfect place to stop for the night.

Using the charts, we found a little-used pier on the southern edge of the island and made towards it. We were careful to keep to the channels marked on our charts and plotter so as to avoid the rocks. Our little-used pier was in fact the parking spot for the Gigha ferry which moored nearby at the end of its day's work. Thankfully, it didn't mind finding a neighbour for the night!

We left as the sun was coming up the next morning. We were out on the sea in the waking world, and the sun hung cool in the eastern sky. It was clear and cold and grey. Above us the sun reached out for the day, below us the sea moved its grey mass into our bow. A pall hung over the Mull; there were no boats, there were no birds, and it was a lonely place to be, so far from the shelter of the shore.

At some point, I put on my life jacket, an instinctive response to the surroundings. We checked and re-checked our calculations; we were satisfied they were all correct but we couldn't be sure. There was no comfort zone. How much is knowledge, how much is experience, and how much is chance?

We drew closer, so small on the waves under the sheer cliffs of Kintyre, an inconsequential trifle on the watery waste. The sea around us changed; it lost the faithful roll of waves. Instead, it had patterns; we saw them forming on the surface and pushed over them.

This was the Mull of Kintyre, magnet for shipwrecks and plane wrecks alike. We had both heard the joke – be careful to dodge the masts of shipwrecks on your way round. The surrounding rocks and reefs have intimidating names; there are long lists of boats that have met their doom by Arranman's Barrels. The Fleetwood trawlers called this part of the ocean the Gates of Hell. The rocks are said to have magnetic qualities that upset compass readings, and for a fair way round there is no reliable mobile signal. It is not unusual for long conversational silences whilst traversing this Neptunian deep, all eyes ever watchful for the unexpected and unpredictable. This was our route to Campbeltown, round these towering rocks that promote disturbance to the natural order and unease in the elements.

I started to feel queasy so Chris suggested that I take the wheel, thinking it might help me to have something to concentrate on. Great rings and watery circles swirled around our bows, unfurling and vanishing. I was tense. Being at the wheel kept my nerves in order and my sickness at bay, but my brain had gone into overdrive. My eyes darted between the charts, horizon, control panels, and cliffs as I tried to keep an eye on the oil pressure and temperature gauges. The unpredictable movements of our boat were disconcerting; I could feel the wood of the deck and frames twist and strain. There was a ridge ahead, a step in the ocean; the approaching sea was all white water. The oak frames juddered. In my hands, the wheel went slack as our rudder pushed into empty eddies, confused momentarily by the lack of speed in the current. The noise from the engine went up an octave and our hearts jolted in panic. Worried that some unnatural power of the Mull had taken hold of our boat, we looked around us for an explanation. To our relief, we saw that the binoculars had fallen from the shelf and the strap had caught on the accelerator lever.

These riotous waters are born from the intense merging of ocean currents that sweep in from the Antrim coast, the Irish Sea, and the Firth of Clyde. The nauseous waters can be further vexed by a westerly swell rolling in from the Atlantic. When we visited the Mull of Kintyre lighthouse and gazed down to the sea from its vantage point high on the cliffs, I was struck by the drama of the place. It is a mass of rock that stands stubbornly, unyielding to the elements. Even on a gentle summer day there is a resonance about it. It is not hard to understand why, in the days before radar, trawlers went round it in pairs, or why in certain states of the tide, a boat cannot make progress against the current and can stay in the same spot for an hour or more.

We had been advised that the safest way to deal with the Mull was to stay very close in to the cliffs, or to stay three or four miles out, thus avoiding the worst of the tidal flow. On this occasion, we had decided to stay close to the cliffs. We had picked up speed, 11 knots, and saw calmer water ahead. The masts dipped and the decks rolled surprisingly but we could see Sanda Island, and some of our stress released. We had been held apart by our individual concentration whilst going round the mull. We came together then, with the ease in tension, and I was able to put on the kettle and make a brew.

Our first voyage: we had done it. We had lived a day in a matter of hours. The voyage provided us with a massive learning opportunity, we had made it round the Mull of Kintyre and now we had some seafaring experience to draw on.

I was exhausted when we arrived in Campbeltown. It had taken all of me to get there, every spare space in my head and every bit of tension in my muscles. I would have fallen into bed if such a thing were possible but, as it was, I instead clambered awkwardly into my bunk and slept instantly. When I woke it was warm and still, voices and sunlight filtered down through the hatch and skylight. I climbed on deck to find Chris in lively conversation with a fellow boat enthusiast.

This turned out to be a continuing roll of conversations that began on arrival and did not finish until mid-evening, making it even a little difficult to eat; I remember this because I was so hungry! One of our visitors was an older man who had worked on our boat during her former life as Wistaria. We invited him on board. He joined us in the fo'c'sle where he sat in his old seat. He told us he could remember sitting in the very same place playing cards or ludo to pass the time – waiting for darkness when the herring would rise, or waiting for their partner boat to return from market. Wistaria was in the north at the time, fishing round the Minch.

I felt warm and safe, and slightly bemused by all our visitors. I think it must have been the crossed masts, so symbolic of the West Coast ring netters, that attracted all the people. I was impressed by the memory and the nostalgia that re-surfaced through the community. Our arrival in Campbeltown on board Shemaron was a day of warmth, welcome, and also of old and fond memories.

Whatever the weather light would spill in splendour....

Shemaron in her languishing state. Tarbert 2007

Shemaron undergoing her first paint fix. Tarbert 2009

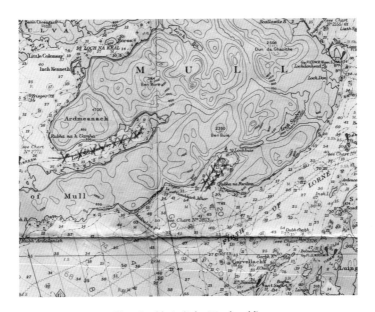

Chart Lochbuie (John Macdonald)

Oak Lea

Billy Sloan looking for herring aboard Wistaria c1960. (H McPhee)

Chapter 6
Over The Irish Sea

We were safely in Campbeltown and our welcome extended through the following day, with more people stopping by to pay their respects to Shemaron. We felt like we had brought her home. In the summer sunshine, the wet and cold loosened their grip on her tight decks, the wood warmed and dried, and it was as though her ring net memories rose on vapours from the shrinking planks to seek out passers-by. Soft whispers carried on the breeze; enticements to conversation: do you remember when...do you remember why? All her wood seemed like a living entity that could not let go of the past. We had learned a lot on our small voyages round and about, and in Campbeltown we began to learn a little more of Shemaron's story. Gently, on vibrant threads of memory, and slowly, in snippets of casual conversation, we saw that Shemaron was opening a new door for us, showing us glimpses of her former life.

Sometimes people were happy just to comment on the weather but more often than not people had a story to share, and that story more often than not would mention Matt or Billy Sloan. When the weather was warm, people would saunter along the quay and chat with us if we happened to be on deck. Other people were happy to stop for a while and sit in the sun to share their experiences. Through these conversations we came to know Shemaron on a more personal level. We were welcomed into the houses of skippers and crew from the ring net era. Between cups of tea, sandwiches, and cakes, we were introduced to Shemaron's former life as Wistaria, and the family to whom she first belonged.

Matt and Billy Sloan were so successful at the ring net that many stories are still told in awe of their achievements. Some say that their great success was due to luck, but coming myself from a self-employed working history I feel sure that although luck may have played its part, there would have been lots of long hours and hard work in between those lucky moments.

This photograph shows the crew of the Wistaria sitting on deck, a sharp and strong-looking band of men, intuitive, focused, and well trained. A primed group. The four tyres stacked by the mast are ready to be used to cushion the boats when they came together to haul herring on board. The piece of carpet lying on top of the tyres was put down on the deck to add extra grip for the crew when they jumped from one boat to another during this process.

Wistaria, c. 1950, Photograph (H. McPhee)

We spent a lovely time chatting with a man who had worked as the cook on board Wistaria in the 1950s. While sharing a generous and delicious helping of scones and jam, we heard accounts first-hand. He told us of times he could remember being anchored in Loch Skipport off South Uist in the Hebrides, and also of times when some weekends, other boats that were finished working would tie up on the quay and their crew would enjoy a game of football. Wistaria however would sometimes stay at anchor in the harbour. I know when we are tied with other boats it can be a complicated task to leave. We prefer whenever possible to leave without other involvement. Anchoring gives us that freedom of choice, perhaps it was the same for Wistaria on those occasions. Watchful and Wistaria worked as partners in the ring net and would sometimes split up and take different routes, change radio channels for secret communications or flash their lights in brotherly code in attempts to foil, confuse or abandon other boats that might be looking to follow and share their luck.

Our experiences with the boat began to revolve more and more around the men who had worked on her. Our voyages were punctuated with pleasant conversation and interest from the people of Campbeltown and Carradale. My bond with Shemaron began to strengthen. Our maiden voyage round the Mull of Kintyre, which preceded our Campbeltown arrival, marked a change in my own relationship with Shemaron; our mutual contemplation had dissipated. Round the Mull we had equal need of each other to get through the confused waters, and so our contemplation had turned to respect. By the time we reached Campbeltown, I felt like our tenuous bond had deepened. We were not quite on speaking terms but we were happy in each other's company.

As the summer of 2011 moved on, we planned to make a small voyage to Ireland in August, and Campbeltown was the ideal place to set out from, so we decided to leave Shemaron berthed there. When we left for Newcastle we felt happy to be leaving our boat among old friends, until our return in two weeks.

A short time later we were united again, a happy trio ready for more adventures. This time we had company for our trip; friends were joining us on their yacht, Sunart. One of these friends had an intimate knowledge of Shemaron, as he was the person who had re-built her engine. His presence reassured us and eased our worry. We rounded Davaar and once again headed round the Mull of Kintyre. The forecast was for changing weather growing more wet and windy. Chris was decidedly on edge. I could tell he was not feeling good about this trip. I think he was battling against some virus and against his senses, which were telling him to stay in Campbeltown.

As we left, the day was bright and warm. Our route kept us well away from the sheer cliff faces and we missed the churning and run-ning effects of the tides that were so dramatic on our last voyage. I sat comfortably on various perches around the deck and relaxed, while keeping my eyes peeled, hoping for sights of big fish. Chris was still feeling anxious and decided to throttle up and get to our intended destination Ballycastle sooner rather than later. With an increase in revs we moved ahead of Sunart, towards the shape of Ireland that was becoming less distinct by the moment. We were leaving the sun-ny sea behind us, and being swallowed by greying skies around the Antrim coast ahead. Any unease in our mood was lost in our concen-tration; going into an unknown harbour is always a little tense. We alerted the harbour master to our imminent arrival but found our allotted spot on the pontoon too small to take us, so instead we had to make for a place on the harbour wall.

I am usually in awe of my husband's boat handling skills, but on this occasion, I think relief at our safe arrival must have somehow affected him in an adverse manner. We turned two complete circles before we managed to bring Shemaron to berth. In the mayhem and to the loud amusement of passengers on the ferry that was patiently waiting to depart, the fish baskets that we had placed at the stern because we felt they lent a certain authenticity to our project, plunged overboard. We eventually managed to tie up, allowing the ferry to make its delayed way out of the harbour.

Understandably tired by this point, I could feel my senses dimming and my bunk calling me to rest, but we had arrived from across the sea and what adventurous spirit I have was also calling me to explore. After the safe arrival of Sunart, we ventured onto Irish soil. We walked among day-trippers and holidaymakers on the sea front; it all felt somewhat otherworldly after our earlier tensions. We found a bench and sat looking rather smugly over the bay, because that was the direction from which we had arrived, from the sea on our boat.

If I thought I was tired when we arrived I was absolutely and completely exhausted by the evening when the general consensus was to head into town. But hey, this was Ireland; there was music, there were pubs and there was Guinness, and thankfully Red Bull, which worked a treat! After a night enjoying the local music, food, and drink we continued in our tourist vein and took a taxi up to the Giant's Causeway. It was a pleasant change from our solitary explorations of the West Coast to have company on our travels, not least because I could sit on board Sunart. This boat had soft cushions and even a fridge from which a gin and tonic would emerge every now and again. She was designed for easier living than our working ring netter, but I had grown used to Shemaron's hard edges and the open spaces below her deck. That evening we left Bally Castle and continued our sea tour with the short hop to Rathlin Island. Ferries had been going to and from the island all day, so we took the opportunity to discover it for ourselves.

Rathlin. What can I say about Rathlin? It is simply one of those places, a place I somehow recognised. It registered with me on some almost imperceptible level although I had not been aware of its existence until we arrived in Ballycastle. I can now look back and remember how I felt without the pressing concentrations of the moment of arrival; I can isolate the sense of recognition, though I cannot explain it. There have been other times during our experiences with Shemaron when my senses seemed highly tuned, it was as if I was reaching for a memory I didn't have. What is it about these places and their haunting beauty? Is it just that there are fewer people around? Does the daily hustle and bustle of congregational life deplete all our energies and leave our senses dulled, masking the magic that is inherent in our surroundings?

We flowed into Church Bay, having crossed from Northern Ireland encompassed in pewtered skies, lustrous light, and calm, calm seas. As we entered the bay, Chris cut back the engine and the atmosphere rolled out to meet us, holding us steady as we glided to the pontoon. We spent that night at Rathlin, an island of caves and the hiding place of Robert the Bruce. Rathlin is an island that can trace its peoples back to prehistory, that through the course of time has been bandied between Scotland and Ireland, but despite this has managed to hold itself firm in its own identity. I would love to return and lose myself in its mysterious landscape one day.

Departure from the lovely Rathlin was a little hastier than

planned due to the turning tide and a sandbar between the sea and us. The next morning we were on our way again to Islay, a little further west than we'd been before. The weather changed little, that is to say, grey skies but dry. There was no wind, so we were surprised when we found ourselves rolling around the sea in our little blue boat. We had caught the end of the changing tides as we rounded Rathlin. Shemaron was rising and falling, joyful in the swell of the churning currents with little or no concern for her crew.

I knew it had to happen; that one day, despite all our careful planning, we were bound to be tossed about a bit, and I have to say it was all quite exciting. It wasn't a frightening experience; it was more that I found it uncomfortable. I think Shemaron was having a ball. I felt it in my stomach, a little question mark. I tried the mind over matter technique – if I don't recognise it, it wasn't really there.

I had calculated that it would take four hours to get to Islay. We had been on our way for about forty-five minutes. I was pretty sure the remaining three hours and fifteen minutes was too long to be playing mind games! I gave in to my fate. I was going to be ill, and accepting that brought a certain calm to my thoughts, which in turn focused on the actual mechanics of being sick whilst stuck in a reeling boat. Fortunately we were able to crank up the engine, clearing the heaving currents quickly and also changing the motion of the boat. The remainder of the cruise was calmer, if a little queasy, and I managed to hold onto my stomach and its contents.

We arrived on Islay and as usual, were unsure where we should be as we were neither a working boat nor a yacht. We ended up over two berths on a pontoon end. Stepping off Shemaron onto land was not a comfortable experience, having found or lost my sea legs, I'm not sure which. We needed supplies from the local store, and I remember stopping to watch as a man who had been fishing from a small boat fed some of his catch to a seal that was launching itself out of the water to grab its reward, obviously enjoying playing to an audience.

After visiting the store, the next couple of hours were spent with our companions who had family living on Islay. They had thoughtfully arranged for the use of transport and generously gave us the grand tour. We passed the Bog Moor; its famous peaty waters are bottled and enjoyed the world over in Bowmore whisky, it is one of the several distilleries on Islay. It was Finnlaggan however, that had called to me from across the sea and for me Finnlaggan was the highlight of our journey. Finnlaggan is a site of special interest with a tourist information centre and a small inland loch. My interest in it bloomed from the treasure trove of memories shared by the older generation of my family.

I was drawn to this place through stories and memories of my granny and aunty, who spent holidays with their family at Finnlaggan during their childhood. They travelled by boat and cart, to laugh by the shore and play under the western skies. Later in life, they were separated from their family by war and boon and never found their way back. My granny remembered Finnlaggan as a farm, but today it is a tourist information point that traces history back to the seat of the Lords of the Isles in the 12th century.

We passed a large house that sat overlooking the loch and continued down the road to the information centre. By this time, it was around six in the evening and the place was closed. We stood awhile in the crystal clear air with the soft smell of Scotland and the sea, but were soon defeated by hunger and the dreaded midge, so took refuge back in the car.

On the pontoons later, it was time for whisky and food. We were leaving for home in the early hours of the next morning and Sunart was continuing her saunter around the islands. We left quietly. Shemaron stepped out from the pontoon with practiced ease. We retraced our steps, passed the landmarks that had lined up crucially on our arrival to keep us away from the rocks. We pushed through the offshore cloud, unable to see very far ahead. During all of this, we stayed on deck. Below deck had become an unnatural and uncomfortable space during our rolling transit, all vibration and noise. We were alone once more on the sea without the comforting sight of land. Sometime later, we spotted the sole white sail of a yacht just visible through the gloom. It was comforting to see another boat. We continued cautiously, picked up substantial knots around the Mull, and were propelled homeward to Campbeltown.

Until this point we had harboured thoughts of returning with Shemaron to Tarbert. However, the warm welcome we received on our arrival in Campbeltown earlier that summer had changed our minds. When we returned to Campbeltown for a second time it felt like a natural home for our boat; we decided to make our stay permanent and have a place on the harbour wall to this date.

Whose Eyes Scanned Horizons?

Whose eyes scanned horizons?
Whose elbow on the wheelhouse sill?
Whose feet on seasoned wood, stood,
Where corks and nets lay on the deck?

Whose moods as fluid as the sea
Read the wind and sky and knew?
Whose hands upon the wheel
Held the engines thrall and began the haul?

When herring rose from the seabed
Who dropped the nets into the tide?
Sole hanging down weighted with lead,
While the boats came starboard side to starboard side?

Chapter 7
Beaching Shemaron

I sometimes lie in my bunk waiting for sleep; I can't see the stove but I see the flickering reflections of flames in the brass handrail and in the lambent glow on the wood. In earlier times, a purpose built light called the winkie may have hung beside the stove. This was a battery light with a mercury connection; it was often stored in the fo'c'sle or engine room to keep it dry. When the ring net was shot, the winkie was attached to one end. Once in the water, it would float to an upright position, the mercury would make contact, and the light would come on. Once lit it marked the end of the net in the water; it was often difficult to see and would appear and disappear on the waves. The name winkie most probably comes from the blinking action as perceived by the onlooker.

The forecastle is such a small space yet it has been touched by so many different lives. The Tilley lamp sways gently and I think about the parts of other lives that have shared this space over the years. What must it have been like having six people living and working onboard? Chris and I fill the fo'c'sle quite well. We are comfortably negligent about our neatness. We wash our dishes once a day, but sometimes this routine slips over to the next morning. If it is cold or wet our chores are done below deck among the coal dust and ashes. Whenever we open the stove door, smoke billows out, adding to the general ambiance we have grown accustomed to.

Perhaps this is one of the less attractive attributes Shemaron has to put up with in return for our guardianship. It would have been impossible for her former crew to effectively manage very much in such conditions! There must have been strict rules about the amount of personal belongings allowed on board – perhaps more of a "minimalist" approach was called for; just enough clothes to fill a locker, or a small suitcase, which could be stored in a vacated bunk. Five other bodies sleeping and living in such a small space – who slept on the top bunks? I have never managed to get into a top bunk and I think this action would require an athletic level of command and dexterity – words I could never use in a portrayal of my husband or myself!

In the working days of the ring net, all Wistaria's crew would be on deck. Night-time was when herring rose and was the most energetic time for herring fishermen. All eyes would be watching for telltale signs of herring shoals. And the expert judgment of the Sloan brothers would be proved once again perhaps by a "burning" in the water. Burning is the name given to a beautiful phenomenon that the dictionary explains occurs as "a result of the bioluminescence of organisms in the surface layers of the sea." When these organisms are disturbed they give off phosphorescence, which is seen shimmering in the water. During the darker hours of summer and autumn, the burning would have been an excellent indication that shoals of herring were around. During the winter, the burning was sometimes seen as sparks in the water rather than a shimmer, presumably because there were less organisms around in the colder months.

Through experience, fishermen were able to draw a surprising amount of information from particular traits in the burning; the movement of a large fish would have a different effect on the phosphorescence than the movement of a shoal of fish. Was there ever some lucky fisherman who saw the Northern Lights in the sky above whilst simultaneously watching the burning in the sea?

Sometimes I would wake to a knock as a gull dropped a mussel or a crab onto the deck, and another beautiful day would begin. One time true to form, our negligent habits failed to spot a packet of firelighters left on the deck when we retired to our bunks. When we rose in the morning gulls had dispersed them. We were never quite sure if they had actually eaten them!

The fact that we can venture upon the sea at our own convenience and take all predictability from our lives always amazes me. In a world in which we have our lives mapped out so minutely on land, I find it fascinating that a few metres offshore, all our normal rules change.

In our sanitized society, where we live within our safe knowledge and reason, our instincts have become subdued and unrecognised. However, out on the sea those instincts can be the key to our safety. At sea we can only reduce risk, and this is not always enough to keep us safely afloat. Instinct becomes an important extra sense; it cannot be learned and must be allowed to mature – awareness brought out from experience. Ring net fishermen developed this instinct. They have honed many skills in their hunting and entrapment of herring: command, dexterity, aptitude, cunning, and ingenuity.

During the early part of 2012, our own skills of cunning and ingenuity were called upon in Newcastle. One of our business contracts was under threat, which in turn threatened the survival of our courier business. It was a difficult time. Our reaction was to try to downsize as much as possible. We panicked trying to sell vehicles and re-duce our outgoings. We were given notice of one month. Our house went on the market, which was heart-breaking for me as it was the place where we had built up our business and brought up our family. It was my security. Then there was Shemaron. Should we keep her? Could we keep her? Could we live on her? Maybe we could move to Campbeltown and make a new beginning with her?

I began to see Shemaron as a possible way forward. I imagined her waiting in the harbour, an oasis of blue wood and happy memories. She was the calm untouched by our storm. My heart ached that I could not forget our troubles and be sitting on her deck, motoring carefree down some sleepy sound. Through the following turbulent months, I carried her picture in my head as a symbol of the peaceful place I wanted to get to. Knowing she was only a few hours' drive away was a welcome comfort. After the initial shock, the thought of changing our lives so dramatically took on certain level of excite-ment. I started to see that the changes we might make could lead to a fulfilling life, one that centred on our boat.

This cruel twist of fate had brought Shemaron firmly into my heart. Over the following months, we fought for our business and to retain our way of life. The one-month notice grew to six months. We took our house off the market and our lives found an uneasy pattern.

However we had more difficult news to deal with. Sadly, after trying to make a fresh start in the Lake District, we heard our friend who had nursed Shemaron through her time in Clyde bank had lost his battle with alcoholism and made a decision to end his life.

We still remember his kindness and his friendship, and think of him often when we are on our boat. Chris has a lovely memory of him onboard, subtly gesturing toward his cigarette packet, kindly not wanting to encourage my husband, knowing that he had "stopped," but aware that he was usually happy to take advantage of an offered smoke.

2012 was a difficult year, it was Easter before I was in Campbeltown again, although Chris had made the journey frequently during our troubled period, in order to run the engine and check that Shemaron was faring well. I think it helped us to cope, having something positive to focus on. With our earnings intact for the time being, we took a holiday let and booked Shemaron onto the slip, in order to check her over properly, clean her, and re-apply antifouling.

We squeezed ourselves into the car along with all the things specific to our intended tasks, and erupted eventually onto the quay at Campbeltown. I stood amongst piles and bags of bedding and blankets, coils of rope and hose pipe, boxes and packages of nails and oakum, and various sizes of pots and cans of paints and oils. The next day work started in earnest. By late afternoon Shemaron was listing helpfully to port, all of the heaviest items on board having been moved to join on that side of the deck: anchors, chains, and vats full of water. By evening, Shemaron had been moved into position on the slip with the much-appreciated help of Sandy. The three of us ate our evening meal on deck as she settled slowly to port, gently finding her temporary place on the wall.

Shemaron stayed safely angled on the slip and we worked well while the tide allowed. I was clad in so many layers to keep warm that it became difficult to move around. I wallowed around Shemaron's lower regions slapping on antifouling paint whilst being very careful not to wade out too far and find the sea invading my Wellington boots. Chris on the other hand didn't bother overmuch; he plodded about in his sea-filled rigger boots, which needed emptying whenever he wanted to be on deck.

We were helped enormously by friends more appropriately attired in dry suits and waders. I never thought much about the actuality of beaching or slipping a boat, and had imagined sand underfoot. As it was we slipped and slithered, tottered and lurched around the weedy slipway trying to find a steady footing before we could seriously apply ourselves. We did in the end achieve a great deal due in no small part to all friends and volunteers. We found nothing to alarm us and were happy everything was in good order. Shemaron was freshly protected against crustaceans of the deep, her keel free to skim through the water.

Over the next few days I found myself slipping into tide time. Our timetables were running an hour later every day. I arrived at the slip one morning to find Chris had bought himself of a pair of waders. He was eagerly awaiting the departure of the sea in order to experience the novelty of working in them. It was cold, wet, and breezy. I had the more comfortable job of painting the gunnels, which meant I stayed on deck. After a couple of hours, my paint pot ran dry, which seemed like a good excuse to call it a day. Sandy had come to lend a hand and I left the two men working, happily bantering in the slack tide.

Later that night, antifouling and waterline complete, the three of us were on board Shemaron again waiting quietly while she came to float. Maybe it was coping with our traumas at home that gave rise to the notion that I was standing in a story: there was a sense of unreality. Shemaron was the catalyst, the propulsion that carried us beyond our troubles. We stirred gently; once again weightless on the water and reversed off the slip, a phosphor bronze whisper in the night arcing across the running orange reflections of the street lamps in the harbour. We circled back skilfully to our new spot on the quay. We tied up as the picture house opposite emptied, and the Irish boats discharged in the brash harbour lights at the end of the pier. We left for bed along with the retiring fishermen and film lovers.

During the ring net era, the crew would spend a few weeks every spring taking the boats out of the water, whereupon they would be painstakingly scraped clean and re-varnished. I have read about an old Girvan ring net boat built by Nobles; this boat needed a few planks replaced, above the waterline. When the job was completed, the owner noticed that the new planks were standing proud of the old ones. When he brought this to the attention of the Nobles' yard, it was pointed out that the new planks were the same thickness as the ones fitted when she was built, and that the "wear" on the old ones was due to scraping.

The scraping would have been undertaken without recompense; after all, if the boat wasn't fishing how could it pay out any money? In Wistaria days, our boat returned home to Maidens and at high tide was taken as far up the beach as possible. As the tide receded, she was allowed to dry out. Stout wooden legs were fastened to her sides to support her without the aid of water. On occasion she would be allowed to settle to one side or another of her own volition. An incident occurred in Girvan one spring. She had been left comfortably settled to one side at the end of the day. When her crew returned the next morning, they found she had re-settled in the tide but had remained bolt upright, precariously balanced on her keel. This prompted the swift placement of fenders under the bilge keel to protect her hull in the event of a topple.

It wasn't until the 1970s that this time-honoured tradition of scraping and re-varnishing was phased out and replaced by a quick repaint in a boat yard. By this time, the boats were working all year round catching prawns and scallops when the herring weren't available.

As a point of interest, one year during the 1950s, Wistaria was painted cream. One theory for this was that when the paint was stripped off at the end of the next year, some light residue would remain. It was hoped this would be enough to cover the dark patches on the planks, which were caused by the corrosive reaction between wood and the metal hull fastenings. The other theory is that she was painted cream simply for appearances. There are few who can remember this, but those who can have commented on how immaculate she looked. She was re-varnished at the end of that year but never painted cream again; presumably this was not a cure for the darkened patches of wood.

The following photograph shows Wistaria discharging herring at Mallaig. It is one of the few pictures showing her painted cream. The wheelhouse door is open and the huge ring net can be seen lying behind the wheelhouse to the stern and partway down the port side. The barrels standing along the quay are for the herring that was sold as fishmeal. Although the herring were freshly caught, if they happened to be at the bottom of the pile in the fish hold, they got squashed and would burst. Herring full of "feed," the term given to herring with full stomachs, became spoilt and were sold for fishmeal. The pictured train carriages are full of prime herring ready to be whisked off to the city markets. There are six carriages on the photograph, with gulls all over them. It is hard to imagine such large quantities of fish.

Wistaria discharging in Mallaig. Painted cream, c, 1950 (Unknown)

In the case of Shemaron, she was always beached on the shore in Carradale harbour. As she moved into her third decade, however, her varnished planks were no longer bright but blackened with age. The darkening of the wood is one of the reasons why these boats were eventually painted. Although Shemaron was one of the last in her generation to be painted, there were other boats that made it into the 1980s in their varnished state.

It is always lovely to hear remembrances involving our boat. One such happened towards the end of September in the late 1960s when she went to fish off the Isle of Man. After a few days of good fishing the weather conditions changed, so Wistaria and Watchful decided to spend a day or two looking round the Clyde. They saw nothing worth shooting their nets for on passage from the Isle of Man, but when they were near Campbeltown, Wistaria shot her net over an area of sea just south of Davaar Island known locally as the Lodan. She caught three hundred and fifty baskets of herring.

Four baskets make up one cran of herring. A cran is the Gaelic word for a measure of herring equalling 37½ gallons, and was used as early as the 18th century to identify a quantity of fresh herring. It may be easier these days to imagine a cran as being roughly equivalent to 28 stone, or about 177 kilograms. Two hundred cran would not have filled the fish holds of both boats, as each boat cold carry in excess of 150 cran, but it was a good amount to take to the market.

Perhaps other boats would have been happy to end their week after three or four good days or nights, but it seems typical of the Sloan brothers and other successful ring net skippers that they were always prepared to push for that little bit extra. This story was recounted to us by the ex-skipper of the Bairns Pride (another ex-Sloan boat that ended up in Carradale) and illustrates the work ethic of Matt and Billy Sloan. This attitude was one of the reasons for the success Wistaria enjoyed during her years with the ring net.

Local tales were even more enthusiastically interspersed with stories of the Minch. There seems to be something about the North that denotes adventure both on land and at sea. These mountainous northerly places rise straight up from the water, holding a sense of the unknown. By rights of age and height, they influence everything that skirts their shores and all that flows around their watery drops as they fall away below the sea. They connect, in one push of magnificent rocky power, the sea, the land, and the sky. The Minch is an area of sea that lies between the Highlands of Scotland and the Outer Hebrides. Flowing over a crater caused by a meteorite collision millions of years ago, it is thought to be in excess of 24,000m deep in places.

The majority of our oceans today remain uncharted. To be surrounded by huge areas of unexplored seas full of question and enigma is such a liberating discovery. That we can venture upon it at our own convenience and in those moments take all predictability from our lives is awesome. There is an interesting observation about the rocks and reefs around Muck:

Above- and below-water, rocks and reefs fringe the coast and there are detached, partly-drying rocks and reefs lying offshore, some of which are uncharted, as evidenced by breaking seas. Mariners without local knowledge are advised to give the area a wide berth.

These insights demonstrate that the sea remains a dangerous place even today with all the improved technology of our fishing era. When fishing round the inshore reefs of the Minch, the judgment of the ring net skippers proved vital for the safety of their crew and the success of their business.

Having experienced the "all aloneness" of being at sea, and the strong connection to nature, I can't help but wonder if fishing for herring in these dangerous waters might have touched some archaic sense essential to our survival. The need to hunt has been a crucial contribution to our path through evolution. Thousands of years ago, farming developed in our communities and reduced the need to hunt; with the herring fishery, adventure remained a part of eating.

It seems appropriate at this point to jump ahead to the summer of 2013, when Shemaron once again tasted the waters of the Minch. She rose up to meet her heritage on the long heavy sea that denoted the change of situation from the sheltered waters and islands. She nudged into the Hebridean Sea. The years fell away in the habit of one who returns after many moons, and the clarity of the memory is unaltered by the passage of time. Still strong and able, her bows rose on the swell and her gunnels rolled with emotion, so near to the historic haunts of her younger, prolific years at the herring.

Where there should have been endless views of the Atlantic Sea, of long spaces and infinite tides, there was only dense fog. Where she expected to be in the middle of oceanic horizons, she found herself in foggy suppression and a smothered view. It strangled sound and stifled the atmosphere and changed the sea in a strange and senseless manner. Shemaron retreated to Coll, a small island to the west of Mull. Chris had broken his ribs when he came off his mountain bike two days before Shemaron left from Campbeltown. Chris was stoically determined, and the journey went ahead, though I think foolhardy might be a term used to describe this decision! Owing to the lack of available rooms on Coll, Chris, trying to seek a little comfort for broken ribs, found himself sitting in the fish hold unable to sleep for most of the long night. Faced with inclement weather and painful ribs the journey to the Outer Hebrides was cut short. Shemaron returned to Campbeltown, with her dreams unfulfilled.

My husband and I have often tried to imagine how it must have been for the fishermen on the Minch. We have read books and tried to stretch the limits of our imaginings. We have touched its fringes and have an inkling of its nature. In the foggy calm of a settled summer it was foreboding, and in the grip of a dark and stormy night, I can't imagine it was anything but terrifying.

Back in her younger days supporting sleek and delicate lines, being built of oak and larch, Wistaria shot her nets, anchored, and sheltered around the bays of the Minch. Partnered by Bairns Pride and Watchful, under the supremely competent Sloan brothers, she hunted round the bays and reefs and weathered the storms.

The pattern of the herring fishery moved clockwise from west to east as the year progressed. The ring net boats would follow this habit and the crew would often be away from home for up to three weeks at a time. I am impressed by the strong connections that were made within the ring net community. Every skipper and crewmember seemed to know personally each and every ring net boat, to whom it belonged, and from whence it had come. Since we have owned Shemaron, we have spoken to a number of skippers and crew who were at the herring. I can hear this connection to sea and community in their reminisces, flickers of nostalgia for ways which are lost and are now vital only through memory; flares of passion like sparks in the winter burning. I am sure it wasn't all "plain sailing." It is the nature of businessmen to keep an edge over the competition, but the big thing was the sea, to which I think they formed bonds like no other.

Through our conversations with the young cook who had worked on board our boat, we learned that when Wistaria and Watchful had finished fishing they would go to market, sometimes together but often one at a time, which gave the neighbour boat a chance to rest and catch up with any running repairs. The catch would be discharged at Mallaig where upon the boat would return straight away to the sea, setting off to meet her partner who would be waiting at some pre-arranged spot on the water.

With gleaming, varnished planks, the partnered boats Wistaria and Watchful waited for each other on the watery deep. They might arrange to meet near some lighthouse whose beams reached out into the night to keep them safe. Night can be beautiful and haunting but also lonely and fearful. Through the altering characters of the night Wistaria and Watchful were often alone, far from the regular night shift. This was their chosen way of life. Imagine waiting lonely on the ocean as darkness smudges the shorelines and all land references are dimmed, watching for the lights of your partner returning. Yet again I am carried away by the beautiful but desolate nature of being alone on the sea; it seems that nothing I write ever comes exactly to what I want to portray but hints only at the essence.

Wistaria and Watchful often met near lighthouses, depending on the area of fishing. One weekend in every four, the skipper and crew would try to get home but journeys were slow and awkward. Work would finish on a Thursday and the aim would be to return by lunchtime on Monday. They never worked on a Sunday. When they were not fishing, they might find shelter and anchor in one of the small bays around Hebrides, passing the time reading or perhaps tackling a crossword puzzle or two. On the occasions when the crew returned home to Maidens, Wistaria and Watchful were left at Mallaig; the Sloan brothers felt the odds for safety were better there than other harbours. This proved to be good intuition, as on one occasion the ring net boats Stormdrift and Fair Wind were blown aground on the island of Kerrera during hurricane-force winds early in the year of 1968, having taken shelter and anchored at Oban.

Chapter 8
The Minch

Our relationship with Shemaron was now in its fifth year. By 2012 we were realising not only the time and effort afforded to our project but also the financial implication. We still felt as though the three of us survived on a wing and a prayer. The purchase and up-keep of wooden boats is infamous for the expense it involves.

During the 1940s and 1950s the costs of building and maintaining boats were just as expensive; Watchful, Wistaria's partner at the ring net, was built in 1959. She was bought for £12,000; remarkably her debt was cleared in three months. At the time, an average-sized house was selling for £2,500.00 with a lifetime mortgage. During the 1950s, a crew member on Wistaria at least once finished the week with enough money in his wage packet to buy a brand new Mini. We are ourselves business people, and struggle on like most other small businesses today. We have had our business for over thirty years and we have never been in a position to buy our vehicles outright, never mind pay our drivers enough to do so. Those were different times, when herring were plentiful and there were good livings to be made.

Our efforts to re-establish the original identity of Wistaria, whilst proving a considerable expense, are cheaper than the costs that a conversion would entail and do lie within the realms of the achievable. Keeping fairly strictly to our plan to restore or renovate as closely to the original specification as possible, we have replaced the rusting water tank with a slightly smaller stainless steel version. Chris took great delight in fashioning a new table top for the forecastle, finding the task of replicating the rough and ready fashion of the original in keeping with his natural style and easier than anticipated. One of our friends later made the comment, "It must have been great to find the original table top, but you must have been slightly disappointed in the quality of the workmanship!"

Holding to our decision to run as closely as possible to 1949 conditions, whilst on board, Chris insisted on the use of a primus stove. I could never get the hang of it. If I didn't pump it enough, everything that touched it would have a sooty residue. If it were overfilled when I tried to light it, the fuel would spill and spread over the carefully crafted table top, chased by the flame. Pretty soon the fire alarm would be blasting, telling the world of my incompetence in making a cup of tea. I was very happy, needless to say, with the donation of a two-ring gas cooker. We placed this in the fish hold, which I believe was the position of the cooker in Oak Lea. I have heard that on at least one occasion, the crew of Oak Lea had to make alternative cooking arrangements when the hold was so full of herring that the little cooker was swamped with fish!

The kind benefactor who donated the much appreciated gas cooker also offered to make a traditional toilet for the boat; we politely declined because we had already fitted a modern flushing sea toilet; and anyway my enthusiasm for all things original doesn't extend to sitting on an old five-gallon oil drum! Our convenience is situated under a particularly leaky part of the deck and even though I sometimes have to pay a visit wearing my raincoat with the hood up, I am thankful for it!

I think Shemaron must have got used to her lonelier status because despite our best efforts, we can never be with her for long enough. She must miss the days when she was Wistaria, part of the herring fleet. Even though the ring net boats were in competition with each other they were all in it together. Housing her original Kelvin K6, a slightly bigger engine than most other boats at that time, and being a few feet longer, she would have hoped for a speedy edge over her competition, and her hold would be able to carry more fish.

There are certain sections on board where I commune more easily with Shemaron, and although these communications are rather one-sided and of course on an intuitive level, I never tire of them. I often sit at her stern. It is a sheltered spot behind the wheelhouse, a strong and steady place to be, over the heart of our boat. The ring net would have sat here, piled in a heap on the deck ready and waiting for a shoal of herring. Wistaria would shoot her net, which was marked at intervals with buoys and its progress over the water would be called to skipper and crew across the night. The end of the net was marked by the winkie, which would be picked up by Watchful. The neighbouring boats would be constantly talking over the radio, easing the procedure along. Wistaria and Watchful joined by their net would then tow for a short period before closing the circle.

An eloquent scenario played out on the waves the as two boats worked as one, every man a smooth piece in the precise process of the motion. I sat at the stern instead of the net, watching the wake and listening. And sometimes I heard something, part of the story rattling in the working notes of the engine.

Shemaron and I were now on speaking terms and I was beginning to see that she had far more purpose than just ferrying me around on adventures. She was built for the ring net, every aspect of her design flowed to this intention. Every part of her was there for a reason; a utilitarian beauty, she was more than the sum of parts.

When I stood on her bow I felt the translation of power as her stern pushed through the water. It was an exhilarating place to be, higher than the stern and more open. It is the point of her mission. It is also the point where the two boats would have completed their circle, trapping the unsuspecting herring and coming together to begin the haul. Wistaria and Watchful would edge together, starboard shoulder to starboard shoulder. Four crew from Watchful would jump across onto Wistaria, bringing with them the end of the net and the tow rope. There is a rope that runs round the bottom of the net called the sole; when it is drawn the net closes and the herring can't escape.

I find it difficult to balance when standing at the bow, so I can't imagine jumping over the gunnels in the middle of the sea, especially whilst in the clutch of darkness. It is hard enough in the harbour when we are securely tied to the wall. The ring net was shot so many times it is little wonder that it evolved into such a fine-tuned and eloquent sequence. Wistaria never knew when she might come upon a shoal of herring. Her success depended on being flexible; her crew had to react as fluidly as the sea that moved around them.

More often than not, because herring come up to the surface at night to feed on plankton, it was the night that hosted this industrious sequence. I have often wondered about fishing at night. If there were no moon it would be a world of shapes and shadows. How did fishermen recognise the shore in the darkness? On a particularly grey day whilst on Shemaron round the coast near Campbeltown, I noticed that I could recognise the shape of the coastline. I wouldn't stake my life on this recognition, but a fisherman would have an in-grained familiarity with his native shoreline. He would know how the land lay between the sky and the sea; he would note the angle of its dark mass in relation to the night sky.

Neist Point Skye. This photograph of Watchful was taken from Wistaria. She is heading north to Polteil Skye. C1960 (H. McPhee.)

On one occasion Watchful was searching by Lochboisdale when she saw a couple of flashes in the water. After changing radio bands, so as not to broadcast his discovery to any other herring boats in the area, Matt Sloan contacted Wistaria to tell his brother he thought he had found a spot of herring. The two boats caught 200 cran of herring and discharged in Oban. Watchful and Wistaria returned straight away to sea and went in search of herring round Lochbuie. They netted a further 200 cran of herring and went back to Oban to discharge. (See chart page III)

At this point it would have been midweek. After further trips crossing the Minch, Watchful and Wistaria decided to take a final look in Lochbuie before the working week drew to a close.

Word had got about that the Sloans were catching herring. Other boats went to Lochbuie to try their luck. As they arrived Wistaria and Watchful were again returning to Oban having caught a further 250 cran of herring. It was Friday by this time, since the market was open until three on Saturday afternoon the brothers resolved to take one more look at Lochbuie.

Wistaria and Watchful returned to the loch, where other boats had been searching for herring. However, after finding none they were resting at anchor. Wistaria and Watchful went quietly up to the head of the loch and caught a further 150 cran of herring. The other boats began to notice what was happening but by the time they roused themselves it was too late.

This story demonstrates a good week in the life of a ring net boat. Wistaria and Watchful were to and fro over the Minch catching herring. It would have taken at least six hours to steam from Oban to Lochboisdale in the Outer Hebrides; a heavily loaded boat would have taken longer. It would take about two and a half hours to steam from Oban to Lochbuie on Mull. Long days steaming, busy nights catching herring, hard work!

After discharging the Watchful in Tarbert (J. Crawford)

The previous photograph was taken after Watchful discharged in Tarbert. There is so much detail in it one can get a good feel for the working boat. Water is gushing from the hose, which is being used to clean the doper lying on deck. "Doper" is another word for oilskin; the name used in this context has fallen into disuse. The brailer (the large round net) is secured to the rigging above the foredeck. The brailer was used to scoop the herring into the hold from the ring net, while they were trapped in the water. The fish hold is still open. The white construction on top of the wheelhouse is the life raft and can be used to tell Watchful from Wistaria in old photographs when the registration number is not visible. The outrigger from the boat almost reaches over the fish hold. Outriggers were lights attached on poles extending from the wheelhouse roof. The ring net winch is situated just in front of the wheelhouse. The anchor is lying up on the foredeck; the long stem can be seen lying over the gunnels. The traditional anchor shape at the other end is obscured by part of a rubber tyre. The end of the anchor is sitting in the tyre to protect the deck from getting damaged.

The old working portion of the boat or more precisely, between the hatch and the fish hold by the step in the deck, is another place I like to stand. It is a vibrant place to be, where I can brace myself against the rigging and actually feel the sea rolling around us. When the crew had jumped from Watchful onto Wistaria, the Watchful would steam round portside. A rope would be tied amidships on Wistaria and attached to Watchful's stern. While the crew hauled in the net, Watchful would pull against Wistaria keeping her steady while the sole was pulled, closing the net. Instructions would be relayed to her and the tension on the rope tightened or slackened according to the sea conditions in an effort to keep the net in its ring shape. In this manner, she would watch over her neighbour, keeping her in position, preventing the herring from escaping, and keeping the net away from her propeller.

Wistaria and Watchful with the ring net, 1959-1963. (H. McPhee)

Wistaria is seen here just in the foreground. Unusually, the two boats had been enjoying some daytime fishing.

Working with Wistaria, 1959-1963. Ring of Herring
being hauled on board the Watchful (H. McPhee)

For the fishermen who lived in Mallaig things were different. They could get home every weekend when they were fishing in the Minch. Leaving around 6:00AM in the winter on a Monday morning or nearer 12:00 midday in the summer months, according to a crew man who worked on Arctic Star during the late 1960s and early 1970s, they would steam across the Sound of Barra to the back of Eriskay where they would ready themselves for fishing that night. (See chart on inside cover) Arctic Star partnered a number of boats at this time: Golden Ray, Castle Moil, and Oak Lea. On the Tuesday morning, if enough fish had been caught, the catch would be discharged at the market. The boats could be fishing perhaps until 10:00AM if the fishing was good, leaving at the last moment to reach Mallaig before the market closed.

Having been up through the night the skipper would set a three-hour watch. On most boats there were crew members who were capable of taking a watch, they would help out so others could sleep. It would take between two and four hours to discharge the herring, then they were straight back out to the Hebrides, hunting for more. At times when the catch was exceptional, both ring net partners would run to market, but more often, one boat would make the journey, leaving their neighbour to rest or perhaps haul the net forward and run a few checks and repairs.

Stormdrift with herring and Thistle both from Dunure, 1959-1963. (H. McPhee)

Oak Lea, mentioned above as partnering Arctic Star in the Minch during the 1960s and 1970s, was a Tarbert boat built by James Noble of Fraserburgh; there are a couple of good pictures of her during more prosperous times in Brian Ward's book, *Tarbert Fishing Boats, 1925-75*. The captions on the photographs give a description of her working life and the following excerpt refers to her in her final resting place against the barn:

> *She left Tarbert in 1961 going to Tobermory then Oban. Her registry was cancelled in 1986 at Kyleakin, where she was beached and left to the elements. She was later placed on a low loader, taken to the mainland, and can be seen today in poor condition lying against the outer wall of a farm steading at Kirkton, near Kyle of Lochalsh.*

It has been an enjoyable task to uncover stories about these ring net boats, and to be able to glimpse moments of life on board them during the times when they were so enterprising and productive. During one of our holidays in Scotland a few years before we had found Shemaron, we came across Oak Lea.

We were on holiday in Dornie when we came upon her leaning against a barn on a farm by the roadside. She looked such a huge thing and so incongruous with her surroundings. She was in a sorry state, her blue paint still visible but flat and flaky, with a tree growing through her middle. She was in a state of gradual collapse, succumbing slowly to decay. She still had majesty about her and dwarfed the barn wall where she leaned.

There was so much about her that expressed her original identity. It seemed as though she had just stopped fishing for a moment's rest but couldn't quite get the energy to return to the sea. In a sad way, it seemed fitting that her wooden skeleton was slowly returning to the earth.

So many of these beautiful boats have been decommissioned, losing the struggle to continue fishing within the strict fishing quotas imposed over the last thirty years and the natural progression towards bigger and more powerful trawlers. They have actually been broken up, ensuring they cannot fish any longer; Oak Lea in her final resting place makes a poignant statement. Long before we came to know Shemaron, the hulking frames of these old boats found a place in my heart. It is with deep satisfaction that I write about our times with our boat, knowing that our efforts have continued to extend her life. We hold her in high esteem as we do the ocean on which she lives. That ocean was to have further surprises for us.

Anchoring in the bays around the coastline of Kintyre has been an experience that has reached into our souls; although just metres from land, the sense of "all aloneness" is vivid. Sometimes when I lie awake in the night and Shemaron strains against the anchor, I hear the wash of the sea on the larch next to my head and I lie listening, softly rocking to the pulse of the elements. The sounds I hear are so remote from my accustomed sleeping arrangement. In my mind's eye I see our hull some distance up from the seabed floating, while an unfamiliar world turns and drifts around our bow. Sometimes we are hidden by the clouds, sometimes watched by the moon and glimpsed by the stars.

Oak Lea

Standing proud your lichen-covered bow rests in green
Awkward out of salt soothed sea,
Against the barn.

Shackled by roots shivering and slithering through your timbers.
Boughs and branches where masts and rigging once flexed and
strained.

Creeping moss clinging on your planks, stretching slow along your sleek
and sinewed lines.

Earth to earth,
Cradling already your splintered shattered frames.

Chapter 9
The Mull

In case we had to sell our boat due to our business predicament, and wanting to get the most out of her before that might happen, Chris and I decided to take a few days away on her in the summer of 2012. We stayed in a hotel for the first night, intending to board Shemaron the next morning. The streetlights came on, marking an end to the evening and the Davaar light spun across the sea, marking the safe haven of the loch. A white cloud hung low over Arran, giving the impression that the lower part floated on the water while the upper was left hanging in the sky. Seals rolled on their backs hoping a morsel or two would fall from the decks of the tied-up boats. The labourers working on the quay finished for the night, unable to continue with the rising tide. We returned to our hotel full of anticipation for the morning and more adventures on board our boat.

The morning proved to be intensely noisy because of the machinery working in the harbour. Semaphore would have been a good way to communicate; we literally could not hear ourselves speak, and we had a hard job waiting for the right point in the tide before we could leave. When we eventually set off, the sound of our engine was a tonic after the constant clattering of the harbour. We made a graceful arc round Davaar; there was a gentle swell on the sea and blue sky beckoned beyond the usual pall that hung over the Mull. We were underway at last, our wake churned turquoise and white, and a steady plume rose from our exhaust.

We travelled through a morphing seascape, where boats on the horizon appeared to be sailing beyond the sea in some other space that existed for a while between ocean and sky. Arran, Ayrshire, and Ailsa Craig were dark smudges drifting off our stern. I sat, binoculars in hand, hoping to see a dolphin or a basking shark breaking the surface. We left behind the greens and browns of Sanda, Sheep Island, and Southend; they in turn morphed and spread to grey beyond our wake, very soon becoming distant and remote. Clad sensibly in my life jacket, I watched the gannets as they flew, refined synchronicity, their wings wide across the invisible updraft on the ocean. I was relaxed and happy; we were on our way at the start of our holiday.

We soon lost the blue sky that had beckoned so promisingly as we left Campbeltown and raindrops started to dot the water. When I looked around I noticed that the surface of the sea was different from our previous escapades around the Mull. There were no areas of smoothness, no forming pools of circular current. The surface was ruffled and tiny wavelets rippled past us. We drew near to the Mull and I joined Chris in the wheelhouse anticipating choppy conditions ahead.

Shemaron tipped and rolled expectantly and the gannets dived into the wash under the sheer cliffs of the Mull. We checked our course, relieved when couple of yachts slipped into our wake; we were obviously all on the same heading. We never felt particularly confident going round the Mull, so this was comfortably reassuring. We looked to the bow and saw churning white water; this was not unfamiliar so we were not too concerned.

Our concentration levels rose as we dipped into the waves. The ocean began to roil around our decks and water foamed all around us. We moved into a trough and watched as the next wave rolled towards us. Disbelief gnawed at my stomach as the moving mountain of water continued to roll towards us and rose high above our bow. We were travelling into a wall of water at 9 knots. Various instructions fought for an ordered sequence in my head, throttle back, never hit a wave head-on – but our deck was already 45 degrees to the sky, wherever the sky had disappeared to, all we could see was a wall of water. I have failed to find any description that comes close to that raw and terrifying moment. Our decks rose, we crashed about the wheelhouse trying to brace ourselves somehow against the walls. We were stunned into silence.

Chris cut back on the engine and wrestled to steer Shemaron by some instinctive force. We tipped upward, bows to the skies. I was aware of a split second when we teetered and then we were falling, careering down the back of the wave to be swallowed in the trough. I breathed, but our plight was far from over. The confused waves were coming at us from all directions; instinct vied with terror as we battled with the elements. Tossed around by such a force we could do nothing but hope to ride out each wave as it came upon us, our minds now absolutely vacant to all but the onslaught of the Mull.

Time slowed, each second seemed to last forever. Chris braced himself against the wheel and I between the window and doorframe, unable to predict, only able to react. In the massing ocean, the bluff of land that marks the North Irish shore appeared and disappeared erratically. On the up surges, we scanned around us hoping to gain a few seconds in which to react. We clung on, unable to reason with our predicament as the mounting sea rolled under our bows. Moving into the swell with the riptide at her stern, Shemaron skimmed the swallows and crested the waves, riding the sea with considered skill, her engine a welcome and comforting sound over the tumult, an indication of her steadfast ability to cope.

Eventually we became aware of Machrihanish Bay off our starboard bow. We were relieved to be on the Sound of Gigha at last. The tumult of the sea lessened and I ventured on deck to find the yachts that had followed in our wake. I spied them immediately, their masts rolling alarmingly round Mull. I quickly suppressed a thought that had sprung to mind: We had been relieved when the yachts slipped in behind us, but now I wondered what they had thought to be ahead. Perhaps they thought they were following a fishing vessel with experienced crew?

Thankfully, our journey continued without further event, though we had to remain alert for the rocks around the coast of Gigha on the south side. Our final tatters of concentration were exhausted following the route through the reefs. Shemaron finally delivered us, two slightly dazed crew, in the calm and beautiful waters around the south pier of Gigha. I am sure she rather enjoyed her journey in the thrall, and was smugly looking forward to resting up beside Silver Lining, a fishing boat we could see tied up already at the pier.

I stood on the foredeck. The crew of Silver Lining called to us that they would be leaving in the early hours, but we were ready to stop and we were stopping here. Nothing would change our mind, no matter how early we would have to rise to help them away. I waited as we inched gently alongside Silver Lining, never quite getting close enough to confidently throw my rope. This was of no consequence, as her crew jumped lithely onto our deck and sorted fore ropes, aft ropes, and springs as they went. We were secure in seconds.

Our day eventually began to mellow. We were keen to see how our neighbours had faired when they had come round Mull earlier in the day. Whilst the skipper did say it was worse than he'd expected, one of the crew commented that he had been unaware of anything unusual. He had been lying comfortably in his bunk at the time! There it was; us feeling like we had conquered the great deep, and them gently amused by our fright.

We were soothed with the setting sun, its final rays casting magnificent colours over the coastline as it fell towards the horizon where it melted slowly from view, pulling with it the remnants of our day. A companionable evening ensued with holidaymakers coming to fish from the end of the pier, look at the boats, or simply watch the changing view. Sometimes we caught a glimpse of the otters that searched for easy pickings from the fishing boats. Out of the gloaming another familiar boat arrived, Ocean Herald, who we knew from Campbeltown. She was also seeking refuge for the night, her deck lights bright in the dusk.

As night came closer the soft communion on the pier dissolved, leaving only the dew clinging in the atmosphere, waiting to settle gently upon the ground. We retired from the land into our cosy foc'sle where we curled each into our bunk (this sounds so lovely, however the process of gaining access to our bunks, although much easier now, was not quite as smooth as you might think). We rolled into our bunks, the sun rolled under our world, and the sea rolled around the few boats roped together on the quay. We slept, rocked in oak, with Shemaron on the night watch, careful of her charges, two childlike souls cradled in her frames, too tired for dreams.

I am always happy to roll into my bunk. When it all gets to be too much and my body aches from the general stoop of life in the forecastle, or when I have hit my head one too many times on the beams, I seek out the only soft spot in the boat. I can stretch out and sink into its comforting hold, thankful that it is soft and welcoming. I am grateful that I do not have to lie on the lumpy flock of a 1950s mattress, although on this occasion I think I would be too tired to care. There were probably plenty of times when a ring net fisherman was also too tired to bother very much about the comfort of his mattress, and his bunk would have seemed just as heavenly as ours did after our fearful trip round Mull.

At some point during the night I was aware of heavy footfalls on the deck and the sound of engines muted through the double skin of the forecastle. I came to a doze much later with wing shadows over the skylight, cushioned on the lilt, and I could hear, just discernible, the squeak of tyres against the pier.

The morning was sublime: warm, sunny, peaceful, gentle, and perfectly restful; Ocean Herald had long gone to her scallops and Silver Lining to her prawns. Our plans to travel further west were thwarted by forecasts of more of the wrong sort of wind. We could have returned through the Crinan Canal or we could have gone round Mull again. As the day progressed, we began to rationalise things. For one thing, the weather, if we left the next day, was no threat. We realised that we had choices too, we could go tighter in round the base of Mull or we could go to the south of Sanda and simply keep out of the way of any rough water. Feeling relaxed and happy we strolled into the village, coffee'd at the boathouse, bought an ice cream, and drank Guinness in the hotel. The sun was still shining when we walked back down the lane, which somehow reminded us of rural Northumberland.

Whilst we were in the hotel, we met an ex-ring net man and spent the afternoon in more pleasant conversation about the old boats. We casually suggested that he would be very welcome to come on board with us the next morning when we returned to Campbeltown. We were delighted and relieved when he accepted our invitation and met us on the pier prior to our departure. He offered to show us a route close in to the Mull that would avoid most of the turbulent waters. The colour of the day was definitely blue, blue sky, blue sea, and blue boat; I did not appreciate this significance at the time. I have since learnt that pagan traditions represent west with the colour blue, this is relevant for no other reason than our adventure was unfolding in the western sea and it was an incredibly bright blue day; the recognition of this older custom seemed poignant. It brought to mind another pagan custom *deasal* – symbolic of things moving forward. The practice of *deasal* involves moving in a clockwise direction, from east to west, pagan custom considered it lucky to move with the path of the sun. It was believed that this direction of movement ensured harmony with nature, I think this habit must be somewhere near the distant origins of the tradition boats observe when leaving harbour, they turn "sun-wise," with the path of the sun. In respect to this time-honoured tradition, we turned clockwise and, in the company of our experienced guest, headed into the day. The plan was to stay close in to the foot of the Mull, avoiding any unpleasantness.

The sea laid around us copper and blue, glinting and undulating; it was such an entirely beautiful day I didn't realise how close to the Mull we had drawn. I could see it clearly, a great rocky bulk in the ocean; it was soothed at that moment by the caressing sea on which we travelled. I could see the sheer rock face, stony and green, and I could feel it. It didn't sit quite happily in its surroundings or maybe its surroundings didn't sit quite happily around it. Almost inspiring, almost beautiful, it lacked the vital essence that would allow either quality to thrive. We grew quiet, a little unsettled, not fully trusting the conditions. It was strange that we were enjoying it all so much considering our last journey round had been so dramatic! The treacherous waters held calm while we passed by.

The pagan custom of turning with the sun to ward off ill fortune used to be observed on land as well as sea; however I have never met anyone who practiced it. It is interesting to note that this custom still holds fast on the water, although the original reason for it has become less clear with time. I have a healthy respect for the pagan religion and sometimes wonder if we have lost some small part of understanding when we left it behind, something that could help us live more harmoniously with our environment today.

The "charmed Islands" of the Hebrides that lie off Scotland's west coast have their share of myth and legend; the myth of the Blue Men evolved from ancient Greek mythology. They are the sons of Glaukos Pontius, Blue Man of the sea, and are collectively known as Glaukidai. The Scottish Blue Men migrated to Ireland from the Mediterranean and are said to live in caves under the Minch. If a sailor saw a Blue Man he could be sure that a storm was to follow. They are reputed to have attacked ships or sailors who had been unkind to Selkies (seal people) or other sea folk. Engaging the chieftain in rhyme could avert their anger; if the wit and rhyme was deemed impressive enough, the boat and its crew would be left alone. Boats often sailed round the Shiant Isles, which lie to the east of Harris in the Outer Hebrides, to avoid the "stream of the Blue Men" or "the current of destruction". Seeing these words on the page, the Glaukidai seem mysterious and fantastical and a long way off, but out on the sea where all our rules change, I wonder if they have a stronger reality.

I came across the following account in an archived copy of the Campbeltown Courier. It describes an encounter with a Bodach, the Gaelic word meaning "old man". I thought it was interesting, as it was set round the ""wee toon"" (Campbeltown) and was more of a local folk tale.

Good folks and honest, it was in the days of the drift net fishing, and never a trall was in it, from the Cowal shore to MacCrummon's Point that on a night o nights a boat from the "wee toon" was at the hauling of the nets, and never a tail in them, but many, heavy was the last of the nets. And when aboard it came, my wonder: on there in the meshes was an old Bodach with a blue fish's tail on him, and he webbed between his fingers like a prize duck. Well: Well: aboard they got him and a fine job they had getting him out of the net – but they got him out, and there he sat glowering at them from the fo'c's'le head. "What's the next move now boys," said the owner of the boat, "for as sure as death this is no canny." So back into the sea they tried to fling the Bodach. Well if they tried, they just tried for round the mast he would fling his arms, and no power would move him. And things did not improve, when at last the Bodach found his tongue. "Aye aye," said he "since I am aboard, here will I remain," and with that he started hammering with his tail fit to knock the timbers asunder. Well, there was nothing for it now but home for them. "Where are you for now," said he. "Home," said the boy. "Not if I know it," answered he, "but to Paterson's Rock," and with that the boat started off like a gannet down the wind. And sure enough they came up to Pater-

son's rock, and an ugly sea running, but the boat sailed right through on top of the rock. At that moment a door opened like a hatch and through it slipped the Bodach as the next serf carried them clear of the rock. And a weary beat home they had of it. Well! well! when they reached "the wee town," and started redding up their nets the last net that the Bodach was in, the meshes were full of real golden scales that he had lost off his tail. "Boys, you and me are the greatest, fools in "the wee town" this very day," said the owner, "for not having cut the tail off him, for it is grand folks we would be this day." But the money they got for the golden scales set them up for life, and after that they had no great notion to be going to the fishing.

There was a time when we lay at anchor just up the coast from Campbeltown; I was roused at odd intervals during the night by inexplicable and strange sounds, which were at odds with the mild lap of the sea. I always found the slosh of the water around our bow quite soothing. On this occasion, even before we slept, we were aware of a knocking sound which came from some place not too far away. We checked our anchor and then all the doors and all our contents below deck and found nothing to explain this irregular and bizarre noise. We kept checking for other boats, which might have arrived in our vicinity but the sea was empty.

The knocking continued all night, but it was the other sound that woke me with a start, like something had hold of our anchor chain and was running away with it across the bay. The muted rattle of trailing links woke me up and I sat up to see Chris already on his way to check that we were not heading for the rocks. I followed him through the hatch. Outside everything was very tranquil; there was

no hint of any disturbance. This happened two or three times alto-
gether and I thought then of the Mermaids and Mermen or other
creatures of Kintyre that had been seen long ago in the area.

Watchful possibly heading north to Polteill on Skye passing Neist Point.
Taken from Wistaria. (H McPhee)

Wistaria Neist Point
(wake from Watchful can be seen in top left of picture) c1960 (H McPhee)

Chart Loch Coalisport. (John MacDonald)

Shemaron steaming - Gigha Sound on her way back from Coll 2013. (D Wilcox)

Fo'c'sle

Postcard late summer 1963. Wistaria is on the outside of the three boats next to Watchful.
(Bamforth & Co.)

Seahouses late summer 1963. Wistaria centre with white tyres on her bow. (Peter Weightman)

Shemaron Ayr 2011. (Finlay Oman)

Seahouses 1963. Possibly the last time Shemaron discharged as Wistaria

Carradale mid 1960s (John Campbell McIntosh)

Scraping the boat. Carradale Harbour late 70s

Lovely deck shot of Shemaron. (KC2000)

Shemaron - Ardrishaig at the end of the Crinan Canal 1970s (J Cresswell)

Shemaron Ardishaig 1970s (J Cresswell)

Tagging exercise 1990. Shemaron was the last boat ever to use the ring net in the Clyde.
(M Foreman)

Chapter 10
Poetical

I have found the Mull of Kintyre to be an extremely inspirational place on land as well as on sea. There is no doubt that it is a force to be reckoned with on the sea. On the shore, the stretches of coast on either side emit a subtle resonance so even on the calmest of days an element of anticipation hangs in the air.

Our dramatic voyage round the Mull knocked our confidence, so we were happy to spend some time exploring Kintyre on dry land. On a hot and lazy day later that summer, we took a drive and stopped by the roadside in the area of the Mull of Kintyre at a point overlooking the sea. We were so high that the boats trawling below us looked like toys moving against an unreal watery backdrop. There was no wind; the day was very was still. It looked as though someone had taken a paintbrush dipped in silver and dragged it in swirls about the sea, silver pathways wound through the flat blue water.

There are so many times when we stop the car and I am annoyed at not having binoculars to hand, so by some amazing act of foresight I had actually remembered to take them from Shemaron and put them in the car. Looking through them I could make out Girvan, Ayr, and nearer, the Pladder lighthouse. After a few moments we drove on, continuing down the steep hairpin bends to Balnabraid Bay. We had stopped here before, but the midges made it impossible to sit for long. This time, however, it was perfect, no midges, no wind, no rain, just clear views and sunshine. I left Chris to close his eyes for a moment on the grassy bank and went for a plouter round the bay. He woke when I returned and we sat a long while soaking up the sights and sounds around us.

The day was bursting with ease. I watched the shallows hoping to see the sleek tipped tail of an otter hunting in the weed. It was getting towards late afternoon and I had seen them before in similar circumstances at that time. A seal popped its head out of the water, a fish jumped near the shore its body twisting in drips of salty brine, but I saw no otters. We rose to return to the car and turned again for a last look at the sea. Not far out, a large shadow was moving swiftly across the bay, and when we looked through the binoculars we realised it was a shoal of fish leaping and playing in and out of the water, moving first one way then another. They were mackerel, which come together during the late summer or early autumn, collecting in shoals before leaving the Clyde.

When herring came up to the surface at night to feed, they could sometimes be heard "playing" in the water. Their tails would be splashing in and out of the sea and would make a particular sound. Sometimes they would jump cleanly from the water and splash back in again, and this would make a different sound, known as a "plout". I have always associated the word plout with pottering through puddles or plodding in and out of rock pools. It was interesting to come upon a truer Scottish use of the word meaning to splash. As with the "burning", experienced fishermen were able to take an educated guess considering the sound and behaviour of a shoal as to the type of fish that swam in it.

So far two of our senses have been identified in the pursuit for herring, sight (watching for the burning) and sound. There are also stories of men who could smell the herring. The sense of smell must have been an extremely important factor in our evolutionary survival. It could be that this skill survived longer at sea than on land, where the increase in industry would overpower natural animal scents. The vast herring shoals of yester-year were so dense and numerous that their smell may have been more easily detectable because of the sheer volume of fish.

During a visit to Tarbert in 2010, when a couple of boats came into the harbour to discharge herring, Chris and I noted a distinctive strong smell and wondered if this was the smell of the herring we had read about in books. Later, after talking to an ex-ring net skipper in Carradale we learnt that the smell referred to whilst looking for herring was totally different, more of a faint musky smell. What we had smelt in the harbour would have been guts and gore. Stories of men being able to smell herring are part of a dimming history. Even in Wistaria days, it was the older generation who remembered such tales, and then the skill was attributed to an uncle or some other person via a link once or twice removed. I wholeheartedly accept this idea. I love any throwback to the past.

We might not readily think of our sense of touch in connection with searching for herring. However, one of the things we discovered on Shemaron was a length of wire wound round part of an old herring box, which had a handhold in it. This was called a feeling wire. The feeling wire consisted of a length of wire 50 to 100 fathoms long, which was wound round the side of a herring box. The wire was lowered into the water where it was weighted by a piece of lead. Fishermen could feel a shoal of herring when fish knocked the wire. The resulting vibrations travelled the length of the wire and were translated by the man on deck who would use his judgement to interpret the information he felt.

Again with experience, the depth and density of a shoal and even the size of the herring could be estimated by the use of the feeling wire. By the time Wistaria was shooting her nets, the echo-sounder was being used as a form of fish detection. However there were certain things that the echo-sounder could not portray, such as the size of individual fish. For a while both the feeling wire and echo-sounder were used in conjunction with each other.

Another account from Tommy Ralston's book, *Captains and Commanders*, is one involving the Sloan brothers, the echo-sounder, and a minister. It recounts how a chance encounter was relayed to profit, despite the superstitious belief that a minister on board was considered unlucky.

After a successful night at the herring, the brothers split their catch between their two boats. They then separated. Billy Sloan went to Ayr to discharge, as Wistaria needed some electrical work done, and Matt Sloan went to Tarbert with Watchful. Whilst he was in Ayr and in accordance with his brother's wishes, Billy picked up Matt's son-in-law, a minister, who had been promised a night out on the boat. The boats and men met up at sea early that evening, and the minster transferred to Watchful. While the men were waiting in the gloaming, Matt switched on the echo-sounder so he could demonstrate how it worked. The echo-sounder showed that the two boats were lying right on top of a shoal of herring, so they shot their nets and filled their holds.

On the subject of a minister bringing bad luck to a boat, it is interesting to note that the Shetland fishermen also considered certain English words very unlucky. Rather than use them, the fishermen substituted them with the closest Norn translation. Norn was the Norse language spoken in a Shetlandic dialect. It survived on Shetland until the 18th century. Some of these old Norn words still survive today in the speech of fishermen, among them the word for minister: "upstarr". Perhaps the superstition of ministers bringing bad luck to a boat has its origin deep in the conflict of basic beliefs between the early Viking raiders and the Christian religion.

Watching gulls and gannets is something we can all identify with and is a more obvious use of our sense of sight. A ring net skipper would watch the behaviour of the birds; diving gannets were a clear indication that the shooting of a net might meet with positive results. I have been told of a particular phrase used by fishermen; when a gannet went into the "hover" position, with both its head and tail pointed downward and its wings flapping, it was said that the bird was "two ply"! I think this is a lovely expression, having seen gannets so inclined on many occasions. Sometimes herring would swim so high that they could be seen "like a film of milk spilt on the water", in this instance they would be completely undetected by an echosounder and perhaps easily spotted with the naked eye.

When a gannet is diving for herring, it enters the sea like an arrowhead, powering straight down to catch the herring, because they swim deep in the water; if it is diving for mackerel, it enters the water at an angle to catch the mackerel that swim nearer the surface. Just off Peninver last year we saw a mass of gulls sitting like ducks bobbing on the waves. It was fairly obvious to us that something was going on in this spot; we scribed a wide circle round the group just for the fun of it, but didn't see anything happening. Perhaps if we had thought to use the feeling wire we might have felt something!

Searching for herring seems to be a remarkably sensorial accumulation of knowledge. How often do we have the chance to develop our senses to their full potential? How satisfied would we feel to have employed them all in the provision of food? The use of our senses makes us complete, brings out the whole man or woman, not just the parts of us required for "modern" living. Ring net fishermen revitalised and used their senses on the sea in ways that were not required on land. They read their seascape; they looked at the sun, moon, stars, and tide, considered all their aspects and acted accordingly. Their practised skill involved a level of interaction with the elements that has been lost today. I continue to be intrigued by this interaction. There must be a whole world hidden in our senses that passes us by on a daily basis.

As partners in a small business, my husband and I have become used to using careful and constructive thought, and the habit of leaving no stone unturned in the venture for a continued livelihood. Fishermen, who also stand at the helm of their business, have somehow managed to weave these skills with the danger and unpredictability of working on the sea, so that they flow together in a current of intention, system, and opportunity.

As every little thing that happened around me whilst I was on board Shemaron was so different from my norm, the situation undoubtedly took its toll. I realised however that although the situation put up barriers, it was necessary to cross them if I wanted to return to the magic that emanated from her decks. What I was coming to realise was that the total experience was so much more than the times of discomfort that ebbed and flowed throughout our trips. My memories were growing; they bloomed and ripened with experience.

I treasured them all, as I could not have the good memories without the not-so-good. I accepted them all as part of the journey to the present moment. I think our sense of adventure originates from acting without the certain knowledge that everything will turn out all right. By taking the leap anyway, we allow opportunities for chance to reveal its unpredictable nature.

We enjoyed more lonely moments on the sea, where the immensity of time and space pressed around us and we were aware once more of our size in comparison to the big wide world. It was during these small times that I think we connected with the world on a basic and ancient level. We were able to bring together all threads of our knowledge and survival, so we could translate them. We had to read and use the elements with the intention of bringing our journey to a happy and successful conclusion.

Our road trips between Newcastle and Campbeltown continued and I always felt that coming into Kintyre was like finding myself in a new world. In early summer, the hedgerows and waysides would wave and froth in a riot of colour, and purple rhododendron would bolt up the hillsides. Flowers that needed so much nurturing to grow in my garden flourished easily on the edges of fields and around rocky outcrops. In the mist, the countryside would soften and moisture would seep through the forests.

I felt the peninsula was full of secrets, a rich landscape of undiscovered histories, biding their time under thick and verdant moss coverings. On the autumn, winter, and spring winds, before the hedgerows abounded with summer growth, I was sure I could feel a difference. Not an unsettling, but a stirring in the land, a release of some slight tension that rose from long-distant echoes.

At the end of the journey our little blue boat waited faithfully, eager for company and adventure. The three of us had become interwoven with each other to a greater degree, washed and bound by the salt and the sea. We joined the line of men and boats, and followed in the wakes of older mariners, storytellers, and poets who found their inspiration in ships and oceans.

During times of danger when the weather perhaps turns for the worse the feeling that boat and man have worked together, faced the danger, and come through it on an equal footing, leads the mariner to identify with his vessel on an almost personal level.

I have found that it is easier to portray our life on board Shemaron if I talk about her as a person. Consider the tale of Jason and the Argonauts, which is set around 1300 BC; the first known written translations of the tale were apparently recorded approximately 600 years later. Way back in the BC years, boats were given a female gender. If we know this was an established custom in those times, it follows that the roots of this custom were set even further back in time. In the epic poem, *Argonautica*, by Apollonius Rhodius, Jason's ship, Argon is given a gender by the storyteller, thus including her in the adventures on an equal footing with her crew. The Argon is clearly a member of the team, risking all in the thrall of the sea.

But as they rowed they trembled, until the tide returning drove them back within the rocks. Then most awful fear seized upon all; for over their head was destruction without escape. And now to right and left broad Pontus was seen, when suddenly a huge wave rose up before them, arched, like a steep rock; and at the sight they bowed with bended heads. For it seemed about to leap down upon the ship's whole length and to overwhelm them. But Tiphys was quick to ease the ship as she la-

boured with the oars; and in all its mass the wave rolled away beneath the keel, and at the stern it raised Argo herself and drew her far away from the rocks; and high in air was she borne.

It is interesting to note the mention of "Pontus" in this excerpt, which may be the same Glaukos Pontius mentioned in reference to the Blue Men in the previous chapter. I have read that Pontius is sometimes portrayed as a member of the Argon's crew, who helped her through many fearful predicaments. In this version of the poem however Pontus is seen in the volatile sea, perhaps stirring up the waves, as more recent legend suggests.

Heimskringla is a chronicle of sagas about the kings of Norway, written during the years AD 850 – AD 1177, a few thousand years nearer to our own time. It uses fierce animal imagery in its descriptions of Viking ships. I grew so involved with the image and rhythm of these verses that I could hardly draw my eyes from them. I have included two quotes for good measure.

Under the heaven's blue dome, a name
I never knew more true to fame
Than Rognvald bore; whose skilful hand
Could tame the scorners of the land, –
Reginald, who knew so well to guide
The wild sea-horses through the tide:
The "Mountain-high" was the proud name
By which the king was known to fame.

The warder of great Odin's shrine,
The fair-haired son of Odin's line,
Raises the voice which gives the cheer,
First in the track of wolf or bear.
His master voice drives them along
To Hel – a destined, trembling throng;
And Nokve's ship, with glancing sides,
Must fly to the wild ocean's tides. –
Must fly before the king who leads
Norse axe-men on their ocean steeds.

In more recent times the poem by Henry Wadsworth Longfellow, "The Building of the Ship", continues this tradition. Even before the boat is built the poet gives it life by bestowing upon it the art of the narrative.

Build me straight, O worthy Master!
Stanch and strong, a goodly vessel,
That shall laugh at all disaster,
And with wave and whirlwind wrestle!

The poem, "Seeker Reaper", written by George Campbell Hay about a fishing boat, is a brilliant illustration of the movement of a boat on the sea. The boat is given a gender and her character and hunting prowess is enforced by referring to her as "a hawk" and "a solan".

These poems, all from different times, convey the same sentiment. They illustrate the manner in which wooden boats respond to the elements in the wind and on the sea. I have felt for myself the flexing and giving of timbers as Shemaron pushes through the confused water. It is as though she has a mind of her own and she is using it to communicate with the sea in order to ease her passage.

To the layman, logic dictates that a wooden boat should be as stiff as possible in order to be strong. However, perhaps the flexibility instilled into the build by skilled craftsmen is one of the many ways that has allowed wooden boats to enter into the heart and soul of the mariner.

Whether story, poem, or real life, the sentiment is the same. I found myself like others before me on the edge of new experience. The thrill of it was in my bones and words clamoured in my head searching for patterns that would convey the right sense of it all.

Chapter 11
Weatherheads

The ring net was first used in Kintyre, as early as the 1830s; our decision to keep Shemaron in Campbeltown was influenced by the fact that in Kintyre she remained close to her ring net roots. This ring net method of catching herring by encircling shoals was more efficient than the use of the drift net; which, as the name suggests, drifted in the water trapping fish when they swam into it. Much larger quantities of fish were caught with the ring net, and increased catches meant changes to the boats. Boats began to change to accommodate the new method of fishing. New designs had covered decks and allowed for the addition of a winch, which made easier work of hauling the herring on board.

The first modern ring net boats arrived in Campbeltown circa 1921. These canoe-sterned boats bear a striking resemblance to Wistaria, who was built twenty-eight years later, and indeed influenced fishing boat design for the rest of the 20th century. These first boats were named Falcon and Frigate Bird. The name Falcon symbolises strength, speed, and hunting prowess; likewise the name Frigate Bird, the silent bird of the sea, gliding effortlessly on thermal currents, has strong connotations of power. Through these hauntingly potent images that link the forces on the sea with forces on the wing, we can imagine the boats moving with the same speed and prowess as the hunting birds. These boats bridged the gap between the traditional skiff and the latest innovations of the time and were the direct forerunners of Wistaria.

Wistaria began life on the East Coast at the Weatherheads boat yard in 1949. Early in 2013 we visited the yard in Cockenzie. Our trip up to Cockenzie was inspired by the re-discovery of a postcard showing Wistaria and her neighbour, Watchful, in the ring net, together in Whitby during 1964.

I was surprised at the size of the boat yard. It was much smaller than I had expected. For me, industry today always conjures glossy corporate images – everything has got to be multi-this, multi-that, and global to boot. The yard was of course perfectly sized for building boats such as the 55 foot Wistaria. When we arrived at the yard, the tide was out and the sun was up. We started poking round the ramshackle buildings of yesteryear with the intention of taking some photographs. It was warm and still. I walked down to the beach following the rusted steel rails that had first caught my attention. I tried to imagine how Wistaria would have looked when she was launched and her hull hit the sea for the first time. Her success in the herring fishery, then later as a scallop dredger, and presently as our project renovation, is a testament to the quality of her build. She is a strong boat and has enjoyed a career of sixty-three years so far.

We walked to the top of the street and turned right into the garage, which now operates from the old Weatherhead yard. The present occupants were happy for us to take a look around and left us to investigate. We spent a few minutes soaking up the grunge and grime of broken boats, silent winches, and redundant rails. Closed off to the sea by massive corrugated metal doors, the yard reverberated to the beat on the radio, a happy and productive space for today's small industry. The huge winch that had possibly lowered the newly built Wistaria towards the water was still in situ and two sets of rails ran the length of the floor until they disappeared under the doors onto the beach. In an unused area of the garage the detritus of scrapped boats, planks, hulls, and giant rusty nails was jumbled in a pile. Around the edges of these bits of ex-boat there were incongruous scatterings of soft down from the current feathered friends who were cohabiting in the roof space.

It was always easy to imagine Wistaria the finished product because we had seen so many old photographs of her: visiting the old boat yard made it easier to imagine the whole boat building process. Locally sourced oak was crafted into the ribs or frames that would support larch planking which, in its turn, would be carefully shaped and curved under steam to render a perfect carvel alignment. This design created strength in the main body, speed in the sleek keel and held the lines that give Shemaron the beautiful shape that still attracts the eye of a fisherman. During our many tasks on board Shemaron, Chris had occasion to drill a hole through the deck. The sharp resinous smell that emanated from the aged wood was still strong after sixty-odd years.

Weatherheads was one of the longest surviving boat yards on the East Coast. The introduction of the government's grant and loan scheme at the end of the war ensured the continuance of their boat building industry by assuring affordability for fishermen during post-war depressed conditions. After the war, every man who returned home was guaranteed a job.

The authority administered low-cost loans and grants to go towards the cost of building new boats. The scheme was designed to help because some fishermen came home to find their boats not fit for purpose after lying neglected during the years of hostility. The scheme also encouraged new ventures.

A huge number of ring net boats were built during the late 1940s in various boat yards across Scotland. The years after the war saw costs for the general equipment required for the day to day work of a fisherman rising to ever higher levels; the price of fish was twice what it was before the war but the cost of catching it was several times greater. The situation resulted in many fishermen finding themselves unable to cope with spiralling costs and looking for a way out of their financial arrangements. This circumstance led to a glut of boats on the market in the 1950s. These boats were available for second-hand purchase; sometimes they could be bought for as little as the sum of any outstanding debt. This fact didn't seem to fit. The stories I had heard about Wistaria's early years were generally of success. The fact that some men were able to make a successful living during these difficult years shows yet another facet to the life of the ring net men during the 1950s.

Further help for fishermen on the West Coast was enabled by the formation of the Highlands and Islands Development Board in 1965. The board supplemented the grant and loan scheme, giving fishermen the means to obtain boats, either new or second-hand. Six years later the board had helped to employ 850 men on 235 boats. Indeed some of the ring net boats from this era are still working and providing a living for fishermen today.

In some situations after the war, as in the case of the Sloan brothers, men were able to return to make up a "team". This happened if they had connections with boats that were able to work throughout the war period, they would possibly re-join a financially stable team who had continued to prosper due to adequate stocks and the fixed price for fish during the war. I sometimes forget it was only four years after the end of the war when Wistaria was built.

One of the special things about writing a book of this nature is having to allow time to recollect and recognise feelings, events, and connections that although in the past, have influenced our present in ways that seemed at the time so random and utterly unconnected.

Holidays seem to be the connecting theme in our story: as a husband and wife with a young family we sometimes chose to spend our holidays in Northumberland, the county in which we live. It always proved a relatively stress-free time, when we would make short journeys to cosy cottages, usually in the hills but sometimes also in the Yorkshire Dales or of course beside the sea.

One holiday whilst staying in Berwick with my sister and our children, we took a short hop across the border to St. Abbs. We had a plan to walk to St. Abbs Head. The day was green, red, deep blue, and incredibly vivid. We trailed along the top of the pink sandstone cliffs, following the path as it dipped to the sea and climbed upwards again to the cliffs. It was one of those places that left such an impression on me that it is always easy to recall. In some way I think it influenced a chain of events. On a separate occasion Chris had stopped at St. Abbs and noted ring net boats Favourite and Fortune preparing to leave the harbour. The sight took him back to the day of his boyhood harbour ride on Boy Danny years ago in Campbeltown. He realised then that he was witnessing a dying fishing culture. Chris and I had found St. Abbs separately at different times but it proved to be a pivotal place in our Shemaron story.

We came to know Fortune and Favourite quite well and often

called in to see their skipper; we were always made welcome. We sat in front of the fire, which either sat ready in the grate awaiting a match or was already burning comfortably in the living room when we arrived. The men would talk enthusiastically about the fishing while I happily listened. We hold fond memories of these times. The friendship offered by the late Peter Nisbit and his wife Libby became a sure stepping-stone along our way.

As our children grew and became more independent, we were able to enjoy more days out round the East Coast. We could break away from our routine and the fetters that bound us so tightly Monday to Friday. Another of our favourite day trips took us up the coast to Leith. On the journey back, we would call in at all the small fishing villages down the road. Fisherrow was still a vibrant place though devoid of much fishing, Cockenzie was slipping unchecked through its past vitality and Port Seton still had its fishing fleet. St. Abbs somehow managed to cling on to the past with its ageing fleet of wooden boats. However, since those times all the larger boats have left.

Chapter 12
Ayr

We had often thought it would be fitting to take a trip to Ayr and pay our respects to Watchful. However every time we were in a position to do so, the weather would play havoc with our plans. We spent a lot of time in bed-and-breakfasts or hotels. Then one lovely hot weekend (in fact, I think it was probably the only hot weekend of the year 2012), we made it across. The whole journey was gorgeous and as usual, our journey up the road was notable.

We eventually left the trails of glinting traffic chains and found ourselves alone. The road was bordered by banks of bluebells and mounds of gorse. Fern stalks nodded in the wind, their fiddle-like heads unfurling in the early summer. There was a frisson in the air, the wind was up and the countryside seemed energised after the subdued spring. White horses were running on the loch, which was all vitality and animation. We ate steadily into the miles, the car engine smooth as silk. Islay, Jura, Rathlin, and Gigha were hazy across the sea. There was so much light; it streamed from the sky and saturated the coast, making everything blue and green.

The weather had softened my arrival on Shemaron. I was comfortable at once, and the forecastle was warm and dry. There was none of the love/hate banter between Shemaron and myself, which often ensued upon my arrival as the fumy interior and hard edges of Shemaron's fo'c'sle overlay the memory of my softer comforts at home. Learning to embrace the smell of oils, fuels, and bilge made the whole settling-in process much quicker. I slept soundly, tipping on the tide.

We left around 8:00 on Saturday morning, moving slowly out from the quay. A gust of wind caught the bow and Chris throttled up briefly to compensate. A gull, engulfed suddenly in the resulting thick brown smoke, wheeled in an instant change of direction. We turned slowly and headed out, passing the Radiant Morn, CN258, and other fishing trawlers tied up on the quay for the weekend. Our bow struck the middle of the sun path on the loch. We set course for Ayr, which took us on a soft curve around the southern coast of Arran. The sea was rolling and sent frothing cascades of spray over the life rings on the wheelhouse roof. It occurred to me somewhat belatedly that in a rocking and rolling sea, I would not have a cat's chance in hell of getting to the life rings should the need arise. We were learning from our previous mistakes, so every little thing was battened down securely.

I stood for a while grasping the rail for balance, exhilarated in the wind, and occasionally gasping in the spindrift. We were passing just south of Pladda Island off the south coast of Arran when Chris saw something he took for a dolphin in the water. It was a choppy sea and everything in the way of the sun was sliver tops and black troughs; I couldn't make anything out. I continued watching over the starboard gunnels and right there in the ebb of a wave was an animal, its black body gleamed in the dark sea. When it came up for air, seawater streamed from its flanks and its back rolled endlessly as it disappeared once more into the deep. What Chris had mistaken for a dolphin was a Minke whale. Fishermen sight Minke whales from time to time but until this point I had never seen one and indeed, although I live in hope of another close encounter, I have only seen one other at a great distance. The steady roll of the whale was quite different from the lazy gait of the basking sharks we had seen. The whale moved with a purpose driven by its need to break the surface of the water and breath. I felt a little ashamed that until that moment I had thought of whales simply as big fish, they clearly are far greater animals than I had appreciated! To see a living whale in its natural surroundings with the wind on my face and our engine running as Shemaron herself rolled on the waves was fantastic!

After a reluctance to hold steady in the confused tides leaving Campbeltown, once we had passed Pladda it was as though Shemaron recognised her bearing. We were heading towards the Heads of Ayr. Shemaron held her own with little input from the wheel, as if the precise degrees of direction of travel were etched into her timbers. She set her course for her old landing grounds, for home.

An hour or so later the sea calmed and we were able to pick out the landmarks of Ayr harbour in the distance. We slowed up, unsure of what to expect at a new destination, and slowly entered the quiescent, empty space. We moved up the channel with its industrial echoes of days gone by, when they say it was possible to walk from one side of the harbour to the other on the decks of herring boats. We tied up as close to Watchful as we could get. It was possibly fifty years since these boats formed their successful partnership as a pair of ring netters skippered by brothers Billy and Matt Sloan. We had arrived and were able to hail Watchful, our consort, as she sat sadly, held fast on her plinth.

Our boat would often come to the fish market in Ayr, her hold brimming with herring. She would have found her place beside the other herring boats jostling or bobbing in the water and fought for the best price for her fish. In the 1950s Ayr harbour was the hub of the community; so many people were involved in its day-to-day business: the skippers and crew, the fish buyers and sellers, the boat builders, and a host of local customers and consumers.

The herring fishery was a massive operation and, whilst I accept we cannot live in the past and that life inevitably changes and moves forward, I believe there is a richness that needs to be recognised in its heritage. So there we were, two lonely boats with a rich history tied to a lonely quay, which was part of an even richer heritage. Partners from a bygone era, Watchful standing as a monument with no explanation as to why she was there and Shemaron supporting her legacy against a mounting tide of disregard.

Chapter 13
Down the
North East Coast

Alongside all the adventure ran a will of steel. My husband and I were united and focused in our efforts to partake in the Shemaron experience. We kept uncovering small stories in her history.

During her career, Wistaria would have neighboured Virginia, Bairns Pride, and Watchful. The boats would have set out from the Clyde and travelled through the Forth Clyde for the fishing off Whitby on the northeast coast of Yorkshire. As a point of interest: shortly after Watchful was built, she would become one of the last boats to go through the canal. Sometime after her journey through, another boat became stuck and did not move for several weeks. This unfortunate event caused people to lose confidence with the Forth Clyde Canal and take a much longer route through the Caledonian Canal. The herring season on the northeast coast lasted from August to September. The following photograph shows Wistaria and Virginia among other boats dried out in Seahouses harbour. It was probably taken on a weekend when the skippers and crew had left, to return home by road or rail.

Seahouses, 1950s, Wistaria centre shot next to the old Fifie and Virginia BA 20

The journey through to the fishing grounds on the North Sea, although undertaken sometimes, was not necessarily a regular event for Wistaria. One of her journeys through the Caledonian Canal took longer than expected; she arrived at a lock just as the lock keeper was finishing for the weekend. Keen to begin the weekend, the keeper refused to open the lock and disappeared. Wistaria was stuck until Monday morning when he returned to work. There was nothing for it; she had to wait it out. It would have been a bit of a hike that weekend for the Sunday paper!

We have pieced together information that gives a picture of the West Coast ring netters at Seahouses, Whitby, and Grimsby. Most of the herring fishing from Seahouses was undertaken along the south side of Longstone Island. It would take about twenty-five minutes to get across from the harbour. This short journey to the hunting grounds meant that boats were often waiting for the right tidal conditions, or, the slack water before they could shoot their nets. Slack water is the term given to the time when the tide is fully in or out and there is no tidal pull. Depending on when they were ready to discharge, they might have to wait again for the tide before they could re-enter the harbour.

On the occasions when herring were not found in the usual places, crew from the Seahouses fishing fleet often helped their Scottish visitors, showing them other places to search and pointing out safe places to shoot their nets. There is an interesting difference concerning which side of the boat the East Coast and West Coast men fished from. The West Coast men fished from the port side; this meant that this side of the boat would be kept clear of fenders for ease of hauling in the net and also for ease of coming alongside the neighbouring boat during the hauling process. The East Coast herring boats would fish from the starboard side. This explains why all the fenders were only down one side of these boats.

Wistaria, 1963 (with the white fenders on her bow)
just before she was sold to Carradale. (Peter Weightman)

The herring season was a busy time for Seahouses; it is obvious from the number of boats in the harbour that there would have been quite an impact on the village. The pubs and shops would have been busy places, alive with engagement. Not all crew returned to their families at the weekend, some of the younger men would stay on board the boats and enjoy the dances on Friday or Saturday nights. There was a certain harbour hospitality, local fishermen might go on board a visiting boat and light a fire, providing a warm welcome for a returning crew at the beginning of a new week.

The two previous pictures clearly show large numbers of fishing boats. I was surprised when a local ex-skipper from Seahouses told me that he could not remember a time when there was any trouble or accident on the water – especially considering that herring fishing generally took place in the dark with only rudimentary lighting. He shared this memory of the ring net boats arriving in Seahouses:

When I was growing up in Seahouses, and it came to the herring season, I remember my father saying that the Fisherrow ring net skiffs were coming that day to fish from Seahouses. We would be at the pictures, we had a cinema, and when you came out about eight o'clock, some would have come up past the Farne islands and some would be in the harbour. It was a great sight. Then gradually the West Coast fishermen would arrive a few days later. That was the start of the herring fishing at Seahouses. You would get salesmen from all over coming to buy the herring and also the transport to take it away.

We made a voice recording of the late Jackie Shiel who fished from Seahouses before and after the Second World War, in which he reminisces about the ring net boats coming down from Fisherrow. He credits the Fisherrow men with bringing the ring net to Seahouses. The Fisherrow boats had been regular visitors for the herring since the earlier drift net era. He also recalls fishing out of Whitby on Good Fellowship, whilst partnering Cluaran.

Cluaran was a Carradale boat and is mentioned in a poem by Naomi Murchison, "The Alba Goes Out", written in 1939. I find myself once again considering the whole poetical picture inspired by the ring net era. From the vantage point of a person who has fallen so completely for an old ring net boat and also who enjoys writing poetry, it is curious to look back and find references to the ring net, recorded in verse, seventy-five years earlier. I have found my way through the present day decay of old boats to a point in the past where I am freshly inspired by the poetry that surrounds them

Jackie describes a few days of ring net fishing thus. On the Thursday evening, Cluaran successfully shot her nets on a spot of herring in the North Sea. Having hauled the fish on board, the two boats went to discharge in Grimsby; they were the first two boats in the harbour the following Friday morning. They landed their catch and by the afternoon they were straight out again. They shot their nets again that evening off Flamborough Head. They discharged in Whitby on Saturday morning, before heading home to Seahouses for the weekend by road. Sometimes they would catch little or nothing at all, other times they could be out at 6:00 in the evening and back by 10:00 or 11:00, with full holds.

Wistaria also visited Whitby. Whitby is situated on a large wide bay; on the postcard in the picture section on page VII, Wistaria is sitting near the top of Whitby harbour where she would dry out protected from the onslaught of any inclement weather. There was space for about thirty boats under the bridge at the top of the harbour; if a number of boats came in together it was a free-for-all to get the best position.

Some of the fishermen in Whitby set quotas for landing fish; this meant that only a certain quantity of herring could be discharged for the market. The Sloan brothers often had amounts in excess of these quotas and preferred to discharge in other harbours, sometimes in Grimsby, Hartlepool or perhaps North Shields.

The year 1963 was the last time Wistaria and Watchful were on the northeast coast together. We know this because later that year Wistaria was sold to the Galbraith family in Carradale. On page VIII there is a photograph taken in September 1963 showing Wistaria in Seahouses. This photograph is especially poignant as it provides part of a picture catalogue of the very last time our boat fished under the command of Billy Sloan, (the postcard shown on page VII of Wistaria in Whitby was taken a day or two before this photograph). Leaving Whitby that summer she went to Seahouses to spend the night, before a planned trip to Cockenzie to collect a newly built boat, also called Wistaria.

The Sloans were replacing Wistaria with a slightly larger boat, which they also named Wistaria. However, at this point the new boat was not quite ready and arrangements had to be made to collect it later.

September 1963 marks the end of the Wistaria and Watchful partnership. Wistaria went on to new things in Carradale while Watchful continued fishing with the Sloans. Eventually, she was sold on for further fishing and ended up in later years as an exhibit in a dry dock in Ayrshire harbour. It is a sad and lonely vigil that she keeps after such an illustrious past.

We have come to the end of an era; under new ownership Wistaria changed her name to Shemaron and moved into the second phase of her fishing life within the embrace of the Galbraith family.

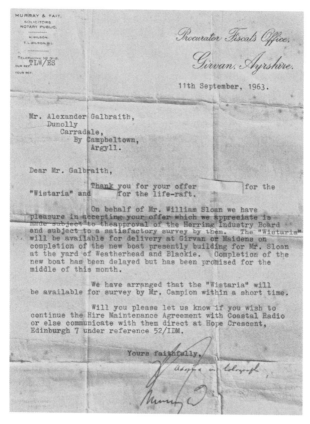

This is the original formal acceptance of the offer for Wistaria. It states that completion of the new boat Wistaria II has been delayed but it is promised for the middle of September 1963, at which point Wistaria was available for delivery at Maidens of Girvan.

Chapter 14
Carradale

Carradale is a small fishing village that lies on the east coast of Kintyre overlooking Arran. We have visited often, taking Shemaron up the coast to her previous home while enjoying the short steam from Campbeltown.

One day we went for a walk along Carradale Bay, where we fell in step with a local man who had been at the herring. While our feet crunched over the shells of dead sea urchins and crabs, our conversation turned easily to boats. We talked of east winds and how several herring boats used to take shelter at Waterfoot, a tiny safe haven situated at one end of the beach. This small bay dries out, so when the herring boats took shelter there, they would have had to lash together for stability.

The channel providing access to the bay at Waterfoot has since altered course and silted up, though a few smaller boats are able to moor there today. I talked earlier about the custom of turning sunwise from east to west; in this little bay I have heard tell of a few staunch believers who, despite the ease of turning westward, turned east as tradition dictated. Sometimes they would get clear but sometimes they would end up stuck on the sandbank and have to wait for the tides to lift them off again.

As we continued to talk, I realised that I had seen this man before in a photo, sitting with his crew in the forecastle of his boat. I had been leafing through one of my husband's books and had stopped at this particular photograph because it showed a fo'c'sle very similar to the fo'c'sle on Shemaron. Coincidently we learnt that we knew his brother, who we in fact bumped into about half an hour later at the harbour. The two brothers owned Florentine, a boat that was fishing from Carradale with the ring net when Shemaron first arrived. We took heed of their advice about east winds and the best places to anchor in the bay and returned the following day on Shemaron. Unfortunately the east wind did not abate; it was one of the more uncomfortable nights in my bunk.

I have more pleasant memories of the summer of 2013 when we arrived in Campbeltown, full of verve to get on with some much needed maintenance on our boat. However, having hit so unusually on a perfect spell of hot settled weather, we neglected our maintenance plan and enjoyed a stunning week anchoring round the bays of the Kilbrannan Sound. The late spring bluebells had faded into the roadsides which blazed with the flowers of summer: yellow iris, deep purple foxglove, rhododendrons, and buttercups. The ferns had uncoiled and were covering great swathes of land with a bright fresh green.

The sights and sounds of the harbour moved in their normal routine as we watched from the sidelines, sitting quietly on deck. Flocks of gulls flew in the wake of Northern Irish boats, Starlight Splendour and Sapphire Stone, as they came down the channel to tie up and discharge their catches on the quay. The glossy backs of harbour seals glistened in the water.

With dark clouds to my back and a brighter sky to the sea, I watched the ferry passengers disembark, disappearing to other destinations. This last flurry of industry marked the end of the day, and the harbour was left listening to the calls of gulls and the sound of diesel engines that never switched off, keeping the boats ready for a quick start in the early morning. I woke often in the night. The effects of a damp boat and the increased heat from our stove created a sauna-like state in the bunks, but when I expertly rolled from my sleeping quarters in the morning, I was pleasantly surprised at how good I felt.

We headed into the swell on the Kilbrannan Sound and rolled contentedly along watching for creel buoys; it was an easy sea on a soft day. Although it was warm there was a certain dampness in the air, which gave the hazy edges of land a yielding quality, as if we could nudge into some point along the shore, pressing ever so slightly into the rocks, until they gave a little and remoulded themselves around our bow. A couple of happy hours later we eased with a calm dignity into Carradale Harbour to find it full with working fishing boats tied up for the weekend. We gently tied up ourselves to settle for the evening. We felt very much at home nestled beside the other fishing vessels along the harbour wall.

Later, after meeting friends in the local hotel, we stepped from the warmly glowing lights of the bar into the night. It was like walking into a watercolour painting; the stillness seemed overwhelming to my normal urban state. I was surprised by the silence; it seemed strange somehow in among the houses for it to be so still. Even the wind held its breath as we made our way down to the small harbour to find Shemaron waiting motionless in the quiet. We had to climb over other boats as we made our way back and it was like stepping through a painting's frame, some kind of border between two domains, as we crossed onto our floating deck.

It rained in the night but stopped at some point during the early morning and the sun slowly burned away the heavy cloud cover. The moist wood and our efficient multi-fuel burner were still creating a sauna-like atmosphere below so I went on deck in the sharp morning to enjoy some fresh air. I sat on the bench at the stern with my toes resting on coils of damp rope. Bits of weed clung to the ropes, which had hung for so long under the water. Long stems whorled over the deck drying fast, baked from below by our oven-like fo'c'sle and from above by the oncoming day. One or two broken mussel shells lay about – they must have been a quick snack for the gulls.

The harbour water wavered gently round the dirty hulls of working boats. When I looked over the gunnels it was like looking through old glass into the sky; behind the clouds jellyfish pulsed loosely, and long tendrils trailed behind their translucent bodies.

By 9:30 on Saturday morning the people of the village were about, walking their dogs, cutting the grass, and collecting the paper. It was so still I could hear their greetings from the other side of the harbour. The skipper of Angus Rose must have been about even earlier, because bunting had been tied around the rigging in preparation for Harbour Day. On the other side of the harbour the momentum of the day was pushing forward; trestle tables and stalls were being set up in the car park. The bunting on Angus Rose fluttered, caught in the bustling breeze. Radiant Morn, Guiding Star, and Avalon sat by and watched, work-worn hulls running with rust and other stains from their labours of never ending fishing days. Tyres cushioned their overworked and treasured bows, and their salty scaly guttural flanks snatched a few hours rest as Carradale moved around them.

The next day, we idled out onto the mirror of sea and headed for Saddell Bay. We were by this time totally captivated by our Shemaron world and it seemed the most natural thing to drop our anchor opposite Saddell Castle, haul the cool box from the fish hold and enjoy a leisurely lunch on deck. We threw the leftovers over the side for the gulls and settled with one eye to the point looking forward to the arrival of Sunart and her crew, with whom we had arranged to meet.

We met up with our friends, and while we were enjoying our catch-up chat we spied the dorsal fins of a basking shark a short way off. With the usual excitement that develops on the sighting of basking sharks, we swiftly untied Sunart and went in for a closer look. We circled the bay a couple of times but the sharks must have dived deeper into the plankton-filled depths and we could not find them.

Back at our anchorage point, the early evening was still hot. We had decided that despite our dwindling food supply we would stay put for the night, so we were very happy to partake in a meal conjured from the cupboards, fridges, and cubbyholes of Sunart's galley. While we ate, a swell had rolled in from nowhere, which made us all a little uncomfortable. So we decided to head for the shelter of Campbeltown harbour. We had another sighting of a small basking shark as we left under the buttercup skies and a faded marigold sunset.

After re-stocking our boat and saying goodbye to Sunart, we set off once again and anchored under Kildonan Dun. The sea lifted Shemaron just a little now and then, the sun beat down on the deck, and a group of ducks paddled towards the rocks. I closed my eyes, heaved a sigh, and let my soul loose on the breeze. The sea sparked with light down among the ripples; it was a day when perhaps one thinks that it has all been worth it. When every consequence has been a step along the way, a step towards a certain moment, and that moment is here. It was not a time to think about the future or dwell upon the past; it was a time for living in the heartbeat of the moment.

We were at anchor, rocking on the wakes of passing boats, soaking up the sun, and contemplating quietly. The ruined walls of the Dun were only just discernible above the profusion of green that summer had at last brought on. It is incredible that it still stands; a memory of those who built and lived in it. A crumbling but tangible part of history, solid among the spinning seasons and turning tides.

The sea glugged its salty reach between the fissures of the sharp shore and the sound rolled back to me, becoming part of the music of the day. The creak of the door as it swung on aimless hinges and the ranging notes of birds that sporadically croaked, screeched, called, and sometimes sang around the isle of Ross enhanced the natural ensemble. I was aware that I had become a little hypnotized, dazed by the sorcery of the sea, and I could hardly wait for the night. To watch the tide run away, leaving its secrets swaying in the rock pools, trapped on the sharp rock edges, or singing sweetly on the surge; to watch the sun set behind the hill and wait for stars in the cloudless sky. On quiet days there is a point when the tide turns and the sea comes back – it sounds like a gentle stream trickling towards the land.

Arran stretched its rocky back long and low on its southward edge and the Ailsa Craig was almost lost past the steps that were conjured from the ocean, made vague by the misty layers of changing influences. The twilight when it came was not something easily shared with streets or land, but something that seemed to have an affinity solely with the sea. It was sublime. We watched the summer dark pushing in as it tried to bring on the night; eventually everything turned grey except for the sky, which kept a precious blue over to the east. The history of the dun rose around us, a long-abiding shout through time, and some quality in the night seemed to hold us close to its ancestral presence.

Shemaron ranged slowly around the anchor and chain that held her at ease in the ancient natural harbour. We dozed, rising from our bunks once or twice to inhale the night, a gentle entrancement on a sleepless sound. Little by little, our small cove lost its detail to the shadows and by infinitesimal degrees the sea spun a silken sheen about our bow. A handful of stars scattered the sky above the rigging and a delicate peach glow floated on the night. Without our sight, other senses waked from their slumbering and tuned into the enchantment. Somewhere out on the sea we heard creatures breathing, heavy blown-out sighs a little way off. A bird cried out from the rocks nearby and a luminescence played about the coils of a rope we lowered into the water.

When we rose a final time, the sea was like polished silver and we watched the clouds skim over the water as dawn broke. We had taken our place along the timeline and shared this space with the way-back-when and the long ago and far away. It was a small strengthening of a thread that continues spinning from prehistoric ages.

With the sunrise came the inescapable fact that we were moving on, leaving the enchantment of the night behind in the blaze of a new day. I am not sure what time it was when I poked my head from the hatch. The sun was up and, although still low in the sky, the heat was already bouncing on the deck. We had so easily been seduced into our holiday that many of the chores we had planned to complete remained in need of attention. The washing of the dishes however was becoming more urgent as we required food receptacles for breakfast. This chore usually means lots of boiling kettles and hauling dirty water out through the fish hold in buckets, whilst quickly ducking away in case the bucket knocks against the combing and the scummy contents spill upon one's person. This morning however, we had an excellent idea: on the deck under the force of our high-powered hose, the dishes were blasted clean in no time.

A little while later I was perched on the hatch skimming the horizon through the binoculars. Between two yachts sailing northwards from Campbeltown, the slow, rolling back of a minke whale appeared. Its small dorsal fin was the only break in a smooth black motion that brought its gleaming back out of the sea, stretching through long seconds, before it submerged and vanished.

We had enjoyed a spectacular few days on Shemaron; our holiday was coming to an end and we decided to spend our last night back in Carradale Bay. That evening Escallonia (a small fishing boat named after Shemaron's predecessor, Escallonia CN 110), came alongside and we had a cup of tea. The simple act of drinking tea with friends takes on a whole new meaning when two boats meet at sea.

Escallonia had been fishing for mackerel, which had so far managed to avoid the tempting line she dangled in the water. We tried a line from Shemaron while we drank, but no fish were lured close enough to bite. After a while Escallonia left to try her luck about the bay and we retired to the fo'c'sle and the comfort of our stove; which warded off the slight chill of the evening. We had only been sitting a few minutes when Sandy called from Escallonia to say that he had come across a load of fish "fashing" about in the water and that he had caught plenty of mackerel. He offered to bring some for our breakfast in the morning. We went to bed looking forward to our mackerel breakfast. I cooked them with oatmeal and they were delicious and filling. The breakfast marked the end of our lovely holiday.

We left Shemaron in a relaxed and happy state. After all our hard work and the stresses involved with our guardianship, it was lovely to have had the chance to loosen up and unwind in her embrace. The whole positive experience left us eager to progress further with her restoration. The memories of these good times held us steady through some difficult decisions that lay ahead.

Chapter 15
Moving On From the Ring Net

In September 1963, arrangements were made for Wistaria to be surveyed prior to her sale to the Galbraith family in Carradale. On September 11, 1963 an offer was formerly accepted by the Sloan brothers for the purchase of their boat Wistaria, by Alexander Galbraith. A delay at the Weatherhead and Blackie yard with the completion of the new Wistaria meant that the sale was not witnessed until November 6 that year, though Wistaria may have been delivered to Carradale prior to this date.

The Galbraith's are a well-established family of fishermen from Carradale, Shemaron replaced Alexander Galbraith's previous boat, Escallonia, which was sold out of fishing at this time to become a yacht.

Escallonia, a beautifully proportioned but slightly smaller version of Shemaron, at around 48 ft., was typical of the pre-war Carradale boats.

Shemaron started her new life partnering another Galbraith boat Amy Harris, as a point of interest the fourth Amy Harris is still fishing today from Campbeltown. Among her new neighbours in Carradale at that time were Florentine, Ocean Maid, Bairns Pride (another ex-Sloan boat, referred to earlier), Maid of the Mist, and of course Amy Harris.

As winter approached, the Galbraith family would have remembered March earlier that year when heavy snow blocked the roads. Delivery vans could not get down to Campbeltown or Carradale with provisions, so the boats went to collect bread and other supplies from Tarbert. The Escallonia had been stuck with ice and her rudder had frozen on Loch Fyne at Arrochar. The problems of this cold snap did not repeat themselves the following winter and Shemaron settled in to her new home. Shemaron was substantially bigger than Escallonia CN110 and was able to carry more fish. At this time she was fourteen years old, she still had her varnished planks and she was pristine. Of all the things that may have been remembered about the arrival of this new boat, it was the smell of polish that is recalled most easily.

She must have been gleaming, outside and in, immaculate, spotless. I wish I could have seen her then, freshly spruced for her new owners. It is still a pleasure to polish the foc'sle. I can easily manage to bring a lustre to the ageing bunks and lockers. The brass mounts on the handrails also come up to a beautiful shine, but it is all lost so quickly when we have to leave for home and Shemaron has to wait weeks for more tender care. A slightly jaded beauty, she can still be brought to life with a little company and goodwill. It must have been a pleasure for the Galbraith family to finally take ownership of their boat, especially with her accomplished past and success at the fishing.

After spending the evening at the local hotel in Carradale one summer night, we decided to go down to the harbour. It was about 10:30 and we were in mixed company. It was a pleasant change to get a female perspective on memories of the ring net boats. In the ring net days, after a drink in the same bar we had just left, the girls came down to the harbour to watch the boats leave. It was a still night and it wasn't hard to imagine my own picture of the boats leaving in the half-light. Sometimes the girls would leave also, on board with the fishermen. This was a common occurrence; in Seahouses on the northeast coast, children and holiday makers would also go out on the boats. I suspect it was a custom that grew in many fishing villages. There was a charm about the process of ring net fishing that would have been appealing and engaging to holidaymakers, school children, and the people who lived around the fringes of its industry.

The decks of the ring net boats were wide and generous. There was plenty of room at night for a stowaway or two. It has been pointed out to me that it could be a long night on a boat with "primitive conditions"! When the boats returned during the early hours of the morning, their passengers would disembark. With honeysuckle heavy on the breeze, they would wend their way up the road to continue the rest of their day. The sounds of the engines on these boats has become synonymous with memories of dusky evenings and of the herring fleets leaving harbours all over the West Coast for a night's work at sea. On waking, or in the uncertainty of the dawn, the first sound to penetrate sleep for those on shore may have been the same reassuring engine sounds of returning boats.

Shemaron, c. 1967. Sandy Galbraith in the wheelhouse.

Shemaron discharging in Tarbert, c. 1967.

During her final years with the ring net, Shemaron fished mainly in the Clyde, sometimes catching herring in Port Righ Bay, literally right outside the Galbraith front door. Her new life however was not always quite so comfortable; in 1965, Shemaron had serious engine troubles. A letter from the insurance company states:

It was reported that whilst Shemaron was fishing in Kilbrannan Sound, Firth of Clyde, on the night of 28th September 1965 a noise was heard to come from the engine and when it was slowed it stopped. It is also reported that on examination the engine was found to be excessively hot in the way of the crankcase and when the crankcase doors were removed it was observed that there had been excessive heat in way of the forward end of the crankshaft. The vessel was the towed to Girvan by Amy Harris CN203 for examination and repair.

The insurance cost for the repair of the engine totalled £1,118.79. In the days of shillings and old pennies, this is a staggering amount when we consider that the average annual income at that time was around £1,260.00

The ring net eventually gave way to the pair trawl, which became the preferred method of fishing. Pair trawling and ring netting did not go well together. Whenever pair trawlers were working, the shoals of herring were dispersed and fragmented which meant that the ring net boats couldn't get a decent catch. When they worked the same patch of sea their different methods sometimes caused problems – pair trawlers would commit to a course for quite some distance while ring netters crisscrossed the area, able to shoot their nets more readily.

On one occasion when Shemaron was fishing west of Pladder Island, off the Arran shore, and two pair trawlers were some distance off, a problem occurred when the ring nets were shot over the pair trawling area. One angry boat steamed aggressively towards Shemaron and actually made contact with her bow! A barrage of aggressive shouting ensued, "You seem to have inadvertently caught our fish!" or something to that effect.

Boats designed for the pair trawl were bigger and more powerful, and by using deeper nets they could trawl for longer periods. They had less of a romance about them than the ring net boats. The relatively light proportions of Shemaron and similar boats didn't really suit the heavy nets needed for the pair trawl. Many of the 1940s ring netters tried, but overall it was the heavier built boats that were successful at it. Shemaron tried her hand with this technique for a while, alternating between the ring net and the pair trawl during the early to mid-1970s. An alternative way of earning a living was eventually found in dredging for scallops. Scallops were becoming a popular dish in restaurants and possibly were more lucrative than herring. For a while, Shemaron alternated between scalloping and the ring net, eventually settling on dredging for scallops by the late 1970s. As she moved into her third decade, her planks were no longer bright but set with the black of age. With the change to scallop dredging and with beautiful new blue paintwork, Shemaron branched out from her ring net roots.

The early 1970s was the beginning of my husband's holiday era in Kintyre. The family's Morris Oxford negotiated the hairpin bends that wrapped themselves round the coastline between Campbeltown and Carradale, full of excited young Malkins. The family would stop at Campbell Stores to buy ice creams before heading down to Carradale harbour. Today, Campbell Stores no longer exists; the building has been turned into a restaurant. It is very likely that Shemaron and my husband may have come across each other during this time. However, not being formerly introduced, they carried on with their lives unaware of the impact they would eventually have on each other.

Shemaron passed from father to son comfortably by degrees. As the years moved on Mr. Galbraith Senior passed the task of skipper to his son, Sandy. Under the ownership of Sandy Galbraith, Shemaron continued fishing for herring and scallops until she was sold out of fishing in 2006 after an almost unheard of fifty-seven-year span of fishing. This action created the opportunity that marked the beginning of our story.

So far it has been quite a journey personally and historically. And only now am I beginning to understand Shemaron. My initial exhilaration has settled, just a little, and I can see her in her natural context. It is as though I was looking through an old piece of glass, grubby with the debris of departed memory. For a time I glimpsed a different life, one that reached out to me from behind its yawning nostalgia, and came to life again through the words of the few remaining ring net men.

I have been caught in a net that drifts on the cadence of voice. My own experiences flow through the gaps while the true strands of the net carry me on the tide of memory, and bring life to my thoughts. I have heard ring net voices, sometimes soft, sometimes strong, often contemplative – like the moods of the sea. Sometimes, almost singing, bringing the whole ring net scenario to a tangible state; so I can almost smell the sea and see the places where the herring swam.

Delving through images of wooden boats and varnished planks brought another dimension to my interest, but there is something in the nature of the ring net men that has added further depth and thirst for understanding. Their passion to ensure that this way of life is not forgotten has spurred me on to record my own findings. I spoke to a man in the harbour one day who told me he was thinking of buying a drift net and trying to catch herring once more from a small rowing boat. What a lovely thought! Perhaps it could be as simple as that and some net fishing could return as an enjoyable part-time occupation.

The Sloan brothers and their father before them along with the ring net have been an inspiration for poets; the herring themselves and their capricious habit have been the subject of poems, songs, and many written words. Fishermen from the Minches to the Clyde endowed individual qualities to the ring net story and succeeded in an industry pulled from the soulful western seas of Scotland.

A young boy who sat in class at Mallaig, overlooking the harbour and watching Wistaria and other boats coming in from the Minch, was inspired to go to the herring. He crewed on the Arctic Star. A writer I know remembers himself as a young boy watching the ring net boats leave Tarbert and lash neighbour to neighbour in Loch Fyne. Perhaps they were deciding which way to go, up the loch or out towards the Clyde. Maybe some were waiting to see which way the successful Jackson family would go in the Oak Lea, so they could follow.

In Seahouses men remember their youth, when they would run out after school to see the Fisherrow boats arriving. In days when journeys by road were a more difficult undertaking than today, boats that came from distant shores must have had a touch of the exotic about them. After a day in a stuffy classroom it must have been exciting to be able to run down to the sea; a sea that never stops calling, so the only question is, what must it be like, to be out there on the waves? I have heard similar stories from Campbeltown; perhaps Boy Danny might have inspired my husband to become a fisherman if circumstances had been slightly different.

The last generation of ring net men, although they did not know it at the time, inspired the last chance for younger men to go to the herring. Once the fishing industry started to change and herring became scarce, men either went on to other types of fishing or left the industry for other employment. Some chose to set down their memories and preserve tradition on paper.

The pathways our boat had shown us led to a door that opened right into the ring net world. The haze of forgotten memory was pushed aside and we saw a whole past existence in all its vibrant texture. For me it is a door that will always remain open. When we are on our boat, it will be held open by the wind and the propeller that turns steady against the tides, when we are elsewhere, it will swing on its hinges, rocked by the turbulences in our lives. Our boat moved on from the ring net era but did not leave it behind. Ring net fishing was the job for which she had been purposefully designed and built, and it will always be her first calling.

Shemaron Dreams

In the cold light of a half moon night
Sitting at the stern.
My weight in open space
Where the ring net lay in layers
Through bygone years.
My weight, no weight
Where the ring net waited ready,
Buoys, corks, sole, and spring
Heavy decked, all checked.
In the cold light of a half moon night,
Diesel running, pushing, turning
Searching for the herring stirring.
Hands on rope, seamless shooting,
Neighbours near, looking long,
Waiting, watching for the winkies blink.
Heavy net, dropping, sinking,
Cold rope, dark sea trapping.
Smooth away, soft sea turning,
Towing, chasing, ring net closing.
Muscles bunching, straining, hauling,
Herring to hold, dripping, squashing.
Engine, steady, gunnels streaming
Markets, sales, harbour steaming.
In the cold light of a half moon night
Emotions rising, Shemaron dreaming,
Soothed on poems pulled from the deep,
Rocks in rhythms on a sea of words,
And returns to sleep.

Chapter 16
A Change of Lifestyle

It is seven years since I stood on the quay looking at Shemaron with a distracted appreciation of her peaceful, grungy looks. After the initial influx of money had gone, we tried to complete more tasks ourselves. We managed to inch forward year by year but we always seemed to have to spend more than we could comfortably afford. During the less affordable times our credit cards took a hammering, but we somehow managed to stay in control; small steps have taken us a long way. The beautiful Scottish scenery and the coastline along which our project grew constantly soothed our stress and worry.

My husband and I have known each other since the tender age of sixteen. Our relationship has had its ups and downs and grown stronger because of them, although I have never quite got used to his casual approach to spending money; my own approach has always been more cautious. Recently I have found that I am more willing to take a risk, and I think my husband has become a little more cautious. We have been working together in a more united manner. Shemaron needs this unity for her continued survival. We have taken financial risks and learned to balance them against our experience instead of against a secure future. I tend towards the optimistic where Shemaron is concerned whereas Chris more often feels the heavy burden of responsibility that comes with owning an old wooden boat. This constant tension is part of what has kept the Shemaron project upright and strong; like a tree that bends with the force of prevailing winds and grows stronger because of it.

A flexible financial framework has allowed us some elasticity in our dealings and we are fortunate to have equity in our house. The element of risk is higher in this venture than in our business, but we have ourselves covered. We have each drawn a line we know we should not cross; undoubtedly our lines are in different places and we keep altering their positions as we force our project forward, but so far we have managed to stay on the right side. We are however aware that we can't keep this up indefinitely and continue to search for circumstances that might lead to a more secure future for our boat.

If life with Shemaron has taught me anything, it is to live for the moment and not to worry about things that may never happen. As my husband and I come to grips with our fifty-something lifestyles, living in the moment is becoming more of a natural state. The stretch into the future that once beckoned with fervent colour and alacrity is shortening every day, and we are learning to look at life from a new perspective. We anchored once under a rainbow on the Kilbrannan Sound and I found myself thinking that perhaps Shemaron was the pot of gold at the end of it: a beautiful, dynamic chancing with debt and doubt but holding strong, ready to shine as soon as the rain clouds disappeared. Each band of the rainbow could represent an experience, colour, smell, or sound that was fresh and new to our lives. Shemaron has added a new ingredient to our life, one that prevents the mundane; I enjoy the lack of predictability our life with her demands.

We have learned many lessons over the last few years. Love and money however were not enough; Shemaron needed time, more time than we could offer by snatching trips between Newcastle and Campbeltown. We needed to create a way of life that allowed us time to give our boat the attention she needed and deserved. After the first flush of money had run out, more work and maintenance had to be attained by our own endeavour. In 2014 we decided to spend a couple of months in Campbeltown whilst working remotely with our business. The plan worked very well; during a prolonged spell of hot summer weather we came to grips with many jobs that were threatening to become overwhelming.

In the mornings I would set up office in the kitchen of the small flat we had rented; this way I kept in control of the paperwork for our business. Chris would walk down to the harbour and start the manual tasks on board Shemaron; at lunchtime I would join him with a simple fare of cheese and crackers or Scottish rolls. It was a happy time. We laboured in the sun while major construction work was completed around the harbour; we were asked once or twice if we were retired. Retired! Far from it.

True, I had once thought that early retirement would be the goal I would strive towards; after all, that is what our parents had aspired to. Since the world financial crash a few years ago, people had to re-assess their situations. I think views are changing. Shemaron is happening now and we want to continue to be part of it. I enjoy all aspects of my busy life and have no wish to retire anytime soon. Our boat has been all about new beginnings; retirement is not in the equation.

Chapter 17
Going Aground

We have skimmed disaster on more than one occasion and have resurfaced gasping but still-committed guardians of our boat. There were many times when insecurity and depression bit deep into our confidence, but it would always rise again after some other person showed an interest in our project or we had a fresh adventure. Then something would happen to make us feel vulnerable and we would once more lose our self-assuredness.

Last Easter, I was on my way to Kintyre. The miles sped lightly by on the start of the soft spring sigh; a gentle inhalation which took with it the ends of winter, then released slowly, waking the iris shoots and tiny white-stemmed flowers along the waysides. I was travelling with my mum. Chris had gone up earlier and work on Shemaron was in full swing by the time Mum and I arrived in Campbeltown. Shemaron had been on the slip for two days, weed and mussels had been scraped from her keel, anti-foul applied round her bow, anodes replaced, and her white waterline freshly painted. Things were progressing well. By Saturday afternoon she was ready to move back into her usual place on the quay.

Campbeltown moved in the indolent mood of a sunny bank holiday and I waited for Shemaron to cross the harbour. It soon became apparent that something had gone wrong. Shemaron had floated off the slip with the high tide as we expected but then her back third caught on the concrete. She was well and truly stuck with the tide about to turn. Her front two-thirds faced a six-foot drop if we couldn't move her before the tide went out. The water in the harbour turned white as Chris tried again and again to find enough momentum to push her keel off the slip, but no matter how hard he tried there was not enough power to move her.

There were plenty of boats around but because of the bank holiday there weren't many crew on board them. I saw a group of fishermen on the other side of the quay and apprehended them with pleas for help. A boat came to Shemaron's rescue, and managed to move her bow to a slightly safer position, but the perilous situation was not averted. By this time I had moved back to the slip and I was feeling somewhat nauseous at the turn of events. I felt guilty that I was not supporting my husband on board our boat, but at the same time relieved that I had both feet on dry land. Chris appeared not to be overwhelmed by the situation, despite the growing audience, and moved in a methodical manner from one failed attempt to the next. Lots of advice was being shouted from the quayside, some encouraging and some not. Despite one or two strongly vocalised comments to the contrary, he believed there was still time to pull Shemaron off if only we could muster enough horsepower.

It was a race against the falling tide, every second counted, it was beginning to look like all our dreams and efforts were about to tumble into Campbeltown harbour. At this point, it seemed as though there was no alternative but to call the lifeboat. As this was being done a larger, more powerful vessel arrived, and with moments to spare, Chris managed to attach a towrope and the slack was taken up. With Shemaron's engine also at full power she slipped into deeper water and safety.

By the time Mum and I had driven back to the other side of the quay, Shemaron was secure in her berth and the small gathering of on-lookers had dissipated. Seeing everything in order, we left Chris to check over the boat for any damage. After the initial relief that he had managed to avert potential disaster, exhaustion set in. Our experience with Shemaron has created a lot of high moments, but it has also created some very low and dark times. Chris felt that he had nearly caused the loss of our boat. I should have realised that after the adrenaline rush there would be a down time, and I should have gone on board to offer support, but I didn't, and my husband felt very alone at this point. Struggling against the urge to simply walk away, he duly pulled up the boards and made sure there were no leaks. Later, we spent a welcome and therapeutic evening in one of the local pubs.

Although this was a first for us, it was not the first time Shemaron had gone aground. In fact shortly after she was launched she went aground on the shore near Portavadie; her neighbour pulled her off the rocks, and luckily there was no damage. We were not alone in our grounding; other boats on numerous occasions had suffered similar plights. I have already mentioned the boats in Waterfoot who got caught on the sand bank whilst practicing the custom of deiseil (the Celtic custom of turning with the sun). Boy Danny, the same boat that had drawn Chris into his love of ring net boats all those years ago, ran aground in dense fog after discharging herring in Oban. The incident weakened her keel, which proved problematic in her later years. Two other boats involved in the same episode were Moira

CN33 and Mary McLean CN193. After voyaging round the Mull of Kintyre and all our other adventures, our worst fears were almost realised in the calm and quiet waters of Campbeltown Harbour!

We were quite shaken after this experience, but important lessons were reinforced: always have two people onboard when moving the boat and never underestimate the power of the wind (or in this case the gentle summer breeze!). When we left for home, it was with unsettled feelings about the project and the risk it involved. It was a low ebb; we had already committed to renting the flat for the summer, and in an effort to upgrade Shemaron's profile we had entered her in the 2014 Commonwealth Flotilla. This flotilla was the largest number of boats ever to make a procession down the river Clyde, it was taking place in July to celebrate the Commonwealth Games in Glasgow. It felt like the pressure was on. The time between Easter and May, when we began our summer stay in Campbeltown, was beset with doom and doubt. However once we had settled into our new routine, the ease of working on board whilst staying in such close quarters made the experience so pleasurable that our waning enthusiasm began to build.

Chapter 18
Balancing Work and Play

The re-surfacing of our enthusiasm was not a smooth transition. At first we lurched between calamity and potential catastrophe. We spilt a tin of blue gloss paint in the fish hold. That led to my first introduction to working in the bilges; by the end of the day we had cleaned most of it away. We ended up with four bin liners full of thick blue slime and soggy paper towels, plus an embarrassing blue line of seaweed that bobbed around in the corner of the harbour for the best part of a week. Anyone who has worked in the cramped depths of an old wooden boat will understand how exhausting this was; after nine hours I was absolutely drained.

On another occasion Chris came close to injury. A navigation light had been left on and one of our two sets of batteries had gone flat. After several hours of charging, a spark from a poor starter motor connection caused an explosion that sprayed battery acid all over the engine room. Very luckily the engine was between Chris and the batteries and he escaped without further trauma. Over the years he has charged many motorcycle and van batteries; he must have read a hundred times the need to ventilate the explosive gasses, but he never thought about the danger in the enclosed spaces of the engine room.

Both these incidences could have been avoided and absorbed many hours of the precious time we had set aside for important tasks.

We were learning and our attitudes were changing. The next catastrophe was dealt with in such a relaxed manner we could have been on holiday. Indeed when I look back on that particular day it is with fond memories, which shows our growing confidence, seeing as how it was possibly the most serious of them all. Shemaron needed painting. We managed this by rigging a floating pontoon alongside; it was roughly 12 feet by 6 feet, and we had to take Shemaron over to the side of the harbour used by the big cargo boats. Chris and I bobbed precariously on this piece of floating wood, pulling ourselves around our boat painting as we went. I did not enjoy this at all, and on the second day I made sure I had my life jacket on.

When the first side was finished, Shemaron needed to be turned. As we slowly moved round, the engine suddenly stopped; it re-started straight away, but a few seconds after it was put into gear, it stopped again. I think Chris realised pretty soon that a rope was trapped round the propeller. We continued with the painting in good spirits knowing that although this was a serious problem we would get it sorted somehow. This was a much healthier attitude: we had begun to trust our own abilities.

By a careful use of forward and reverse gears, literally three or four revolutions of the propeller each way, in the flat calm of Campbeltown Harbour, we managed to inch Shemaron across the water to a corner where she would be safe to dry out with the falling tide. That evening we waited on deck while the tide went out. It was an uncomfortable feeling; we were attempting something for the first time and were less than certain of the outcome.

Walking to the bow was a bizarre experience: I found myself

walking on a downward slope instead of upward as Shemaron settled her bow onto the harbour sand. Things began to fall forward as she tipped deeper in a slow careen. When the life raft fell across the wheelhouse floor narrowly missing my feet, I decided it was time to leave. A couple of hours later Chris put on his waders and walked through the low water to cut the rope and free the propeller.

For some reason I love to remember this night, not only because of its quiet beauty, but also because we realised that whenever something might go wrong in future we could work calmly together to put it right. We returned later in the cold sharp hours to bring Shemaron forward as the tide came in. We did this by pulling on ropes. There was no noise. While Campbeltown slept we pulled, threaded, and tucked ropes round the bumpers of cars parked on the quayside. Thirty-two tons of boat came silently and surely at our bidding, quietly relieved to have been freed from cumber Shemaron, once more returned to her usual position. On a more practical note, we also learnt the importance of carefully stowing our own mooring ropes whist manoeuvring in a harbour!

Our angst always dissipated when we were able to get out onto the water. With the weather set to be still and smooth, we decided to take Shemaron and anchor up the coast to continue our ministrations under the beautiful Dun at Kildonan. It didn't seem that long ago since we were there; it was only the year before during our wonderful lazy holiday when we kicked back and did absolutely nothing except watch for basking sharks and whales. What a day! The sun shone down on us and we painted while Shemaron ranged slowly on her anchor. The tide went out and came in again and we worked on through the day while the rocks grew then shrank back into the sea with the incoming tide. Gunnels, strakes, and strings all pristine and clean!

It was our first time at anchor that year. It was a late start but it was worth the wait. The sea was quiet; we saw a couple of gannets in the late afternoon, and the only other thing we heard were the calls of oyster catchers. It was a very peaceful work environment. We headed back to Campbeltown around 9:30PM. Returning in the twilight was a good chance to check that our navigation lights were working; so far our trips had all been undertaken in daylight and we had never needed to use them.

Although staying in Campbeltown was predominantly about working on our boat, we did manage a few trips out. Staying near our boat made it easy to climb aboard and just go, so one Sunday morning we emptied the contents of the fridge into a carrier bag and went! This time our chosen destination was the Ailsa Craig. We could see it between Davaar Island and the land as we were leaving the harbour, a grey mound topped with lighter coloured rocks.

The day promised to be still, mainly cloudy with patches of sun. After all our manual efforts during the week we felt no qualms about taking the day off and enjoying the ride. Once clear of the channel and the lobster pots, we turned southeast. We lost sight of the Ailsa Craig for a short time but it re-appeared once we passed the Davaar lighthouse. There was a yacht under sail heading towards the mull, but our course was out towards the grey horizon and the mysterious lump of rock that beckoned. We were full of anticipation – heading for a destination by sea is always a thrilling experience, but a destination that can vanish and appear on the whim of the weather is a mystical wonder.

After our attempt to visit the Outer Hebrides in 2013, the rest of our trips on Shemaron during that year had kept us close to the

Kintyre shore. This time we struck out from the coast and made straight for the middle of nowhere, we found ourselves embraced by the circle of the slate grey sea. The wind was warm, a perfect complement to the day as we pushed gently on.

I think we must have confused the gulls when they flew above our deck or skimmed, wings wide, beneath our bow. I am sure they were hoping to find fish. Instead we fed them caramel wafer biscuits. They hitched a ride, and their webbed feet slipped and slid down our freshly painted gunnels. As we got closer to the Craig the gannets came, first one, then another, patrolling from their lonely rock.

We drew closer still, the wind grew a degree cooler, and the sea stopped rolling. In the lee of the Craig the water was deep green and the air was filled with the calling of birds. We realised the white colouring we had thought to be light-coloured rocks was actually colonies of gannets. A choir of them chanted from the Ailsa Craig. Shemaron had once again brought us to a wild and powerful place. There was a potent sense that we had somehow crossed into a different world. Ailsa Craig held that strange sense of the lonely wild and an echo of something primordial in the life of the birds that chorused from their colonies.

Taking time from our work program was a pure delight; the next week we took a couple more days out and took Shemaron to the head of Loch Fyne. We tagged on to a small group of vessels escorting a replica Viking long ship up the loch. With an engine happier at a speed of several knots and tuned for seeking out herring shoals, Shemaron found it difficult to match the pace required by an escort and we decided to move ahead. The fog had come down so thick it was impossible to see any distance off our bows. I stood for a long time on the foredeck watching for the buoys that marked the channel for

Otter Spit, which we expected on our starboard side. I saw them at last and we turned appropriately up the loch. The beautifully restored ex-fishing boat Golden View had followed our lead and because we were ahead of the main body, we decided to take a break.

We lashed the two boats together and had a quick cup of tea while we waited for the viking flotilla to appear. There is an unreal sense about the world when it is covered with fog. It was a relief to be still for a while. Once we had stopped however, the silence seemed overwhelming and the loch was eerily still. It was a novelty for Shemaron to have a neighbour again, as she is so often on her own; as Wistaria she may have often lashed with the Watchful whilst waiting for decisions about a night's fishing with the ring net.

It was a little sad to see the loch that once brimmed with herring and hosted such a profitable fishing industry so quiet. The ring net developed from these shores; Inverary, Ardrishaig, and Tarbert each had their own herring fleets on Loch Fyne. We spent a quiet night at the head of Loch Fyne. Tied to Golden View we turned slowly on the water, enjoying the green backdrop of forested hills in the misty confines of the inland waterway. The two boats moved round slowly, getting to know one another through the gentle stirring of memories, times when their holds were filled with fish after being out on the sea.

The next morning we left the small flotilla and started back down the loch; the sun was shining brightly and it was hard to believe all the beautiful scenery we had missed, when it had been hidden under heavy mist the day before. The buoys we had found hard to locate in the fog on our way up to Cairndow stood out brilliantly and hailed our passage; cars flashed between the trees on the loch side road and Shemaron moved sedately down the loch.

We passed the small islands of An Oitir and Eilean Aoghainn, an area known as the Minard narrows on upper Loch Fyne. Our recent trips had been more often on open waters. It was lovely to be on the loch surrounded by the typical hillside colours of a Scottish summer. We cooked lunch on the little gas cooker and ate it in the wheelhouse as we passed Tarbert. We rounded Skipness Point, and then the Kilbrannan Sound lay before us, our route back to Campbeltown. My growing familiarity with this stretch of coastline meant that I was able to recognise the characteristics of the land that mapped our way home.

After our couple of days away we were refreshed and ready again to start work. Flotilla 2014 was now only three weeks away, and we wanted to have Shemaron looking really, really good! Chris had noticed a fumy smell while we were steaming home and decided it would be prudent to check the exhaust. After years of heavy use the exhaust had grown so rusty that it disintegrated upon inspection!

When Shemaron had worked as a scallop dredger, the engine ran so hard that the exhaust would glow red; this meant that it needed constant maintenance throughout her working life. I cannot say that we were surprised when the exhaust fell off, but the timing could have been better. Progress with our boat took a step backward and the chances of her making it to the Flotilla were looking slim. When the exhaust disintegrated it exposed a measure of heat damage to two of the deck beams, which had to be repaired before the new exhaust could be fitted. It was a long two weeks while we waited for the expert attentions, provided by Campbeltown's engineers and joiners. With every problem we overcame we got to know our boat a little better and our confidence grew. Shemaron had enjoyed a hardworking life; her new exhaust should easily manage her more sedate and retiring lifestyle today. It felt a little weird seeing her with a hole in the deck where the exhaust should have been, unwillingly deprived of her strength and efficiency. It was a relief to get her put back together again, to see her whole once more and stronger than before. We were back on track.

The expense of replacing the exhaust was partly offset by coping with most of the other work ourselves and not enlisting the help of a boat yard. It is always difficult to find a balance between affordability and expense, and we continually try to rationalise our ownership of Shemaron. During our many discussions on the subject, we have tried to justify owning an old wooden boat by comparing our situation to that of someone owning a static caravan; as the expense grew we decided that we might both also be members of fairly salubrious golf club. As time has moved on we find ourselves struggling with the caravan and golf club scenario and think we would be more comfortable with a small cottage! If we can keep our expenditure to £5,000 – £6,000 a year these comparisons work fairly well. If we have a big expense, like, say, a gearbox or engine failure, then things could be extremely difficult to manage financially. I tend not to think about growing expense and focus on our positive experiences. I know that my husband worries constantly and has compared our situation to the oft repeated cliché of standing under a cold shower fully clothed, tearing up twenty pound notes and watching them disappear down the plug hole.

There was little we could do while Shemaron waited for her repairs except enjoy the delights of Kintyre. We witnessed some awesome moonrises. I like the way the moon reminded us of our place in the universe. Standing at the window of the flat and watching the moonrise over Kildalloig Hill low on the summer sunset was quite a spectacle. We went over to Southend a few evenings to watch the gannets flying low across the sea. They seem to fly towards the Mull – perhaps they nest on the cliffs there.

There is a moment just after the sun goes down when the earth seems unsure of its identity, the temperature drops and there is an aroma that hangs in the sharp dampness of the approaching night, a mix of salty rocks, sea, vegetation, and the filtered silts of streams. We had not been able to take Shemaron out as much as we had hoped, but we had an excellent choice of beautiful bays where we could sit watching the sea whilst absorbing our rich surroundings. After one of our evening walks we returned while the sun was setting. There was a certain spot on the road where we could see the glorious sunset over the Isles of Jura and Islay burning red; at the same time over to the east we saw Arran suffused in the pastels of the setting colour spectrum; behind us the moon rose brighter and higher.

Shemaron Saddell Bay 2013

Shemaron Crinan Basin 1997-98. (Darren Purves)

Shemaron working hard 1997-98 (Darren Purves.)

Just painted 2014 Campbeltown

Shemaron with Golden View at the head of Loch Fyne 2014

Greenock Commonwealth Flotilla 2014.

Chapter 19
Flotilla 2014

Our final week in Campbeltown was spent preparing for the Commonwealth Flotilla. We checked routes and tides and listened to weather forecasts. I had mixed feelings at this time; though the flotilla was undoubtedly a brilliant event to be able to take part in and it would raise the profile of our boat which we felt was an important step in her future conservation. But it also marked the end of our most enjoyable time in Campbeltown.

Our trip up from Campbeltown started with a lumpy sea. It was a while before we felt safe enough to go below deck to put the kettle on. Being an old ring net boat, Shemaron's gunnels are very low. This allowed the crew to jump from one boat to another. When the sea is rolling we stay together in the wheelhouse; it is safer and we can keep an eye on each other.

Just venturing out to make a cup of tea can become a perilous enterprise. Shemaron's wide and generous decks have many blind spots and there have been times when I have been at the wheel and a quick scan round the boat has failed to reveal the whereabouts of my husband. A heave on the rusty old Claxton has become our signal to stop whatever we are doing and make an obvious appearance.

Eventually, though, the rolling troughs of our wake softened to gently undulating wavelets and our journey progressed pleasantly, though I am sure Shemaron had enjoyed having her decks refreshed in the salty spray.

New and unfamiliar coastlines rolled out ahead of our bow, and as we turned northeast towards the mainland, the sea settled nicely. The mainland coast was everything, the Ailsa Craig or the head of Loch Fyne was not – busy with sea traffic, for one. The odd yacht or ferry crossing our path was normal on our excursions around Campbeltown, but here we had to take constant note of the yachts, ferries, container vessels, and trawlers that were criss-crossing the water. We felt tiny compared to the container vessels that moved surprisingly swiftly around the Clyde estuary. We passed by Great and Little Cumbrae Isles and to the south side of Bute as we made our way towards Largs. Despite all this action, our run was beautifully uneventful and the sun showered its blessings upon us.

Everything was well. After the couple of weeks of forced inactivity when we replaced the exhaust, we had cleaned up as best we could and had broken the back of our journey. We were at last beginning to relax.

Our plan was to stay a night in Largs Marina before heading into the Clyde and making for Greenock where we would meet the rest of the Flotilla. It was five years since we had first brought Shemaron down the Clyde since the initial work had been completed in Clydebank, and decades since she had fished in the area for herring. It was a lovely feeling, re-visiting the area. Shemaron looked a little conspicuous in Largs Marina; her blue working hull and wide spacious decks were at odds with the white yachts and her size was exaggerated beside so many smaller pleasure craft. She was welcomed with warmth and interest. Her long years of work and her age gave her an individual presence and she attracted attention.

It was one of the hottest summers on record; there were moments when it felt like we were in the Mediterranean rather than Scotland. Being on board Shemaron in these temperatures brought problems we had not yet encountered. We have no fridge, having managed with a cool box and from time to time a donation of ice from one of the fishing boats. Below decks the heat was intense. There was no way we could store any kind of fresh food; we were hungry and finding tins and dried food unappealing, a pleasant place to eat became a priority. We sought a recommendation from the yacht next door; this prompted an invitation to the yacht club for our evening meal, which we enthusiastically accepted.

With our evening plans to the ready I went below deck to freshen up and change. Freshly pressed, I climbed onto the deck and was just about to go onto the pontoon when Chris decided to check the stern gland. This is the part of the boat where the propeller shaft goes through the stern. A few moments later a barrage of the most sincere profanities erupted from the engine room hatch, induced by the discovery of a blocked limber hole. Limber holes are holes in the frames of the boat that allow any water, in this case water leaking through the afore mentioned stern gland, to collect in one or two central sumps; having collected in the sump the water can then can be pumped out. An hour or so later, Chris emerged with a good coating of oil over his face, arms, and fine-figured torso! I was torn between the comedy of the situation and total exasperation. After all our tender ministrations and exalted efforts, Shemaron couldn't even give us one night off. We felt like the parents of a young child with a bad attack of colic.

We didn't manage to clear the blockage but were determined to have our night off; we made Shemaron as comfortable as possible and left her to her own devices. Of course we had to clean and change yet again and the quickest way to do that was to apply liberal amounts of Swarfega followed by a repeated dousing of seawater. Not for the first time I heard Chris lament that we should give it all up and collect stamps instead! That evening after we had cleaned up as best we could, we enjoyed a good meal on the terrace of the Largs Yacht Club. With our hunger vanquished and pleasantly replete we watched the sun go down over Bute whilst swapping boating stories with our hosts.

We arrived at James Watt dock in Greenock the next morning to a very warm welcome from the event organisers and also from people who remembered our boat as Wistaria. Wistaria may have come into James Watt dock to discharge herring in her ring net days. On this occasion Shemaron was keeping more sociable hours than those required for ring net fishing. We were all hoping for a peaceful night to get ready for the start of the Flotilla the next day. We welcomed aboard extra crew who were joining us, friends and family who we had not seen for a while. Our excitement at being reunited added to the energised buzz around the marina.

We gave Shemaron over to our guests for the night and booked ourselves into a local hotel to make sure we got rest before the big day. Suitably refreshed, the next morning we made my way to the marina. There was an excited hum of anticipation on the pontoons, all the boats were getting ready to leave. We were feeling a little nervous as we moved out – it was a big day and very public. We circled round the mouth of the dock while we waited for the other boats to come into the river. As the space got more crowded we moved a little further out. Shemaron was not quite as responsive as some of the yachts that were nearby; we were more comfortable with plenty of empty water around us because we took longer to turn and needed a bigger turning circle.

The flotilla was divided into groups and each group followed their leading boat. Our lead boat was Alba Endeavour and we slid easily behind her as she came by. We were off, making our slow progression up the Clyde. The tight formation was difficult for our boat and it took a lot of concentration to handle her. We had to be constantly aware of getting too close to other boats and other boats getting too close to us.

The flotilla unfolded slowly along the length of the river Clyde. When we looked over the stern we could see the sun picking out white hulls way back round the river's bend. Our crew appeared on deck wearing kilts and drew extra attention from the growing number of people appearing along the riverbank, evidenced by the appreciative whistles that cut through the cheers and Claxton blasts from the shore. We had ended up near the front of the flotilla, which was a massive ego boost; it may be shameful to admit but it was great to feel we were ahead of the pack (even though it was not a race!). We needed these high spots to keep our enthusiasm afloat; the flotilla gave us a great push of positive energy.

From the walls of Dumbarton Castle, onlookers waved and cheered and the banks of the Clyde filled fuller with people who had come down to the water to enjoy the sun and witness a little bit of history being made on the river. It was possibly the largest number of boats that had ever been on the Clyde at one time. We followed the ferries under the Erskine Bridge and we were all caught up in the effervescent atmosphere, responding to the crowds by sounding our own Claxton and ringing Shemaron's bell. It was a brilliant fun-filled day.

We arrived in Glasgow and from our point on the pontoon we had an excellent view of the other boats entering the dock. We waited for our neighbour, the beautifully restored old herring drifter called Swan. We knew Swan from Campbeltown harbour where we had tied up together on a previous occasion. The pontoons gradually filled and transformed into a riot of masts and coloured flags. Loud cheers from spectators watching the games nearby mingled with the general happy hubbub in the dock. It was a day filled with lots of laughs; I think we will all remember it for a long time.

One night was all we had time for – after two months away, home and work were calling. We left Princes dock the next morning in the rain and sounded Claxton as a goodbye to the remaining boats in the flotilla. Soon all we could see was the mass of flags that ran to the tops of the masts still sitting in the dock. The riverbanks were wet and quiet but we still enticed a wave or two from people out for a Sunday stroll or a spot of dog walking. We continued on to Greenock where we said goodbye to our crew and helped to unload their gear. Then it was just the two of us again alone on the water heading for home.

The forecast was for winds up to force five, occasionally gusting to force six. We decided to take a route round Bute, an island in the Firth of Clyde, and keep to sheltered waters. There was a thin gap between sea and sky as Shemaron entered the Kyles of Bute, heading towards the ever-closing space. Eventually it became impossible to see where the sea and sky met, and the Burnt islands were almost lost in the fog. There was only an opaque grey wall ahead. I soon discovered our new exhaust was a comforting source of warmth, leaning on it was like holding a hot water bottle in a chilly bed, and standing behind the wheelhouse, I could stay reasonably dry.

We picked out the buoys marking the safe channel through the Kyles and by the time we cruised round the western side of Bute the weather began to clear. We had thought to stop for the night in Portavadie, the old favourite place from our early voyages, but with the up-turn in the weather conditions we changed our minds and decided to press on for Campbeltown.

We cruised in to the Kilbrannan Sound welcomed by a southward tipping swell. After eight hours we were tiring, so thankfully there were only two more hours to go before we would be tying up in Campbeltown harbour. The weak evening sun leaked through holes in the sky, casting watery rays to our starboard side. Shemaron dipped into the swell and rose on its back. We turned on the radio and songs of the 1960s floated along the sound with us. The sight of the sun after the long grey hours lifted our mood and we passed Davaar in high spirits. After so many hours on board we were happy in the rhythm of everything, comfortable with Shemaron and the sea. Despite being tired, we found ourselves reluctant to bring an end to our journey by climbing on to the quay.

We had enjoyed an amazing two months in Kintyre. Our return from the flotilla marked an end to our time in Campbeltown. During 2014 we notched up plenty more nautical miles and combining our trips with social enterprise created an opportunity for more people to engage with Shemaron and her ring net heritage. When we left Campbeltown in August, I had only seen Shemaron looking smarter in some of the old photographs we have discovered; our efforts brought her leaps and bounds further forward.

If my husband hadn't been interested in fishing boats I am fairly certain I would never have stepped onto the deck of old ring netter. My husband wanted to help preserve these incredible old boats but we never expected to unlock such a treasure trove of experiences. The changing times of dawn and dusk, where the sky meets the sea or the waves meet the rocks, places on the edges of energies that have manifest over thousands of miles, have a powerful pull, and I can feel them all from the deck of our boat.

Chapter 20
Legend?

The period of the ring net marked the beginning of a move towards bigger and more powerful boats; at the same time, it embraced many of the old ways. The epoch that holds the first fishers at its beginning and the ring net at its end, spans a time which amplified a way of life that evolved through a growing understanding of nature.

During my research I have come across one or two interesting links to older languages: odd Gaelic and Norse words have popped up now and again. *Maol*, a rounded hill, is still a good description of the Mull of Kintyre. It can also mean dull or bare, an accurate description of the treeless rocky expanse of the Mull. A more obvious example is the word *port*, a bay, inlet or natural harbour, as in Port Righ near Carradale Bay. These and other examples I have come across appeal to my sense of romance and also to my own habit of continually trying to find a place for myself in a world that often seems to move too fast.

As I understand it, these languages embody a whole different way of looking at life; nature is the prime driving force and the language grows from that. To live a little closer to nature makes so much sense. An essential and intimate knowledge of the shorelines grew into habitual method, which continued through the years in the routine of fishermen and sailors alike. They recognised the dangers of being at sea. The cohesion of land, sea, and growing knowledge blended into a specific fishing culture around our island shores that began to erode with the start of the industrial revolution. The old boats are disappearing but remnants of their culture survive in some of the Gaelic names that identify certain points on the shore.

As a "land liver" I have always thought of the sea as a separate entity. During the compilation of this book I have come to see the land and sea as a single entity. One thing I have come to appreciate, which maybe holds the essence of what it was like to be at the herring, is that the land and sea work together; one cannot be without the other, the beauty and the peril are inseparable. The ring net men were more in touch with this essence.

I recently had the opportunity to witness a small gathering of ring net men by watching footage of an event that took place in Carradale. A small group of half a dozen men had come together for an evening of reminiscing; I had spoken with most of them before and found them to be both entertaining and engaging. They were watching pictures and footage from a private collection of records of their old fishing days, put together with music. As the ring net men watched the pictures move on from days of the ring net to purse seine netting (one of the methods of fishing that replaced the ring net), the camera panned round the room, catching their expressions. The guests became subdued and each person seemed to retreat into deeper and more private thoughts. As they watched the film showing the fishing method that had brought an end to their way of life, expressions of genuine sorrow dimmed their countenances. I had been searching through boxes of old ring net photographs at the invitation of my host when I became aware that a rare moment was unfolding in the recording on the screen in front of me.

I have spent hours trying to understand and write about the ring net story. Every conversation was enlightening, enjoyable, and took me closer through more knowledge and greater understanding. I gained so much from the experience, however, I was not part of the ring net era and so have not lost it. Unexpectedly, the tide of feeling that underlies the memory of the ring net had become a palpable thing; it reached out to me in a final push of tangible emotion. There is a rich story here that deserves to be kept alive in the telling and re-telling. It should be nourished by the sea and given a voice, not relegated to the dusty darkened confines of a museum, or even worse, allowed to disappear completely.

What will they say of the men of the ring net? Perhaps, "There once were hunters on the sea who could smell their prey. They read the wind and stars and embraced the night. They filled their holds with the ocean's bounty, shot their nets under the moon, and moved over the water with eloquent skill. They became part of the night and the first breath of morning". The Oxford dictionary defines *legend* as a traditional story popularly regarded as historical but not authenticated. The ring net story cannot then be a legend for the simple reason it is very positively authenticated; the rest of the description however fits the ring net era well. The men of the ring net have not realised legendary status; indeed I hope this book goes some way to revive a living interest in them. Every time we read about the ring net men or make some comment, a little extra life extends upon the ring net era.

All this thinking provoked by an old wooden fishing boat! I am thankful for it. The whole experience of writing this book has left me primarily with a thirst for more: more adventure, more knowledge, and more understanding. It has allowed me to recognise a space inside myself that is thirsty for life. We will continue in our guardianship of Shemaron, taking our journey with her one day at a time to see how far we get. We have many places we would still like to explore, including more of her old haunts round the Clyde, the Minch, and perhaps the East Coast. We will travel, enlightened by our experiences and enhanced because of the volume of historical knowledge we now hold. We will travel as privileged onlookers to the ring net story. Shemaron will continue to promote her heritage on the water, preventing nostalgia from dragging her too deeply into the shadows.

Far below the contrails and clouds I will watch a plume of exhaust gas trail grey above a turquoise wake, and listen to the clattering noise as the diesel runs. I will lose the straight edges in my life and watch Kintyre find its colours in the circle of the sea. I will see the sun through fanned tails of gulls and watch gannets soar. I will look for sharks and whales and see seals lying on the shore.

In Memory of Greg Ramsay Robertson

"Even as a small boy Greg loved the sea and dreamed of spending his
  life working there."

Gilly Robertson (mother)

Greg Ramsay Roberston
27 December 1984 - 1 July 2002